Kill All the Chickens

For Garret

Kill All the Chickens

Grief and Memory on an Ozark Farm

AMY OLBERDING

polity

First published in 2026 by Polity Press Ltd.

Polity Press Ltd.
65 Bridge Street
Cambridge CB2 1UR, UK

Polity Press Ltd.
111 River Street
Hoboken, NJ 07030, USA

ISBN-13: 978-1-5095-7544-2

A catalogue record for this book is available from the British Library.

Library of Congress Control Number: 2026936299

Typeset in 11 on 14pt Warnock Pro
by Cheshire Typesetting Ltd, Cuddington, Cheshire
Printed and bound by CPI Group (UK) Ltd, Croydon

For further information on Polity, visit our website:
politybooks.com

Contents

1

What I'm Really Saying

Some few years ago now, I set out to write a book that my career had well positioned me to write, a scholarly book on death, loss, and bereavement. I am a professional philosopher by trade and training and have by now spent most of my adult life writing and teaching philosophy. By the time I started that book, I had already published some journal articles nudging up to the subject, articles detailing this or that philosopher's approach to this or that aspect of grief and mortality. With the end of my career closing in, it seemed fitting to go ahead and make a meal of subjects I'd been intellectually snacking on for years. As it happens, I have no stomach for a meal like this.

I did work on that book. Several unfinished chapters, partial drafts, as well as countless outlines, scraps, and fragments are neatly tucked away inside the laptop on which I presently write these words. When one wants to work but can't quite make the work *work*, sometimes it's useful to do a bit of organizing. This explains how all that book material came to sit in a well-organized folder labeled *Stupid*, a folder I have rarely opened since I gave it its proper name. What started as a bid for better organization concluded more like a funeral. I created that folder the way one might a tombstone; I laid a finding marker should I ever want to visit dead ideas. It was the stuff that brought me to abandoning that book on death that stuffs this book.

In my early years as an academic philosopher when I most needed to publish lest I perish, I devised a trick for writing that initially served me well. Having run aground with research I was writing up, I would set aside the necessarily smart-sounding draft I was fruitlessly fettling and start a new document. And then I would fill out that page with whatever muddled idea I was then pursuing but write it in my own voice. I would abandon all effort to sound polished or like one who well knew what she was about in favor of saying plainly whatever it was I had originally set out to say. Or I would say plainly just why I was struggling to say the thing that I had meant to say. In short, I gave over writing like a philosopher and wrote like a person instead. Most of the time this worked to clarify my mind and enable me to return to my draft restored, my scholarly persona back in place as a filter rather than a suffocating, muting muzzle. In this way, almost every journal article or book I wrote had in its background a set of "what I'm really saying" pages, and I managed to keep the flow of academic research going at the kind of clip the modern university expects. This is how a person can end up with a scholarly book on moral role models in early Confucian tradition but also tuck away a prolonged meditation about the hypnotic, graceful efficiency with which Grandpa used to lace up his work boots. That chapter on moral aesthetics was never really about Confucius, I can now confess.

I here intended to write an intelligible introduction to this, my present book. And I am about to do just the thing that started my trouble in the first place. I want not to tell you what this book is about but instead to drift away in gentle melancholic reverie about just how my grandfather laced his boots. When you have work boots with hooks along the top, you rarely need ever to untie the laces. Instead, you just unhook, carrying the tied lace back and forth on the diagonal, unhooking side to side until you're down to the eyelets and can loosen up enough to kick them off. Then, when you need to put those boots on again, you just pull the tied lace tight upright and start a graceful back-and-forth to let the hooks catch them as you go. When you have done this over a long calendar of years, it can start to look like magic, like a ritual dance performed to please the gods of farming. I loved watching my grandfather lace his boots. It is how I now lace my own, though I so far await without answer some sign that the gods are pleased. With that explained, I can recall myself to purpose and to better sense.

When my writing of that book on death and grief would run aground, I did as my long practice dictated: I turned to making "what I'm really saying" pages in a bid to make those needed formal pages come. The formal pages did come at first, though slowly and quite badly. As I had trained myself to do, I kept then retreating to my own voice, writing out frustrations and all the things I'd wish to say if only I could find my way. Soon enough, this is all I seemed equipped to do. In retrospect, the reasons for this are surely several, and at least some are circumstantial.

If you want to write a scholarly book on death and loss, best not get underway just when a global pandemic arrives. For some, I suppose, this might concentrate the mind, but for me it was not so. This, too, owes much to circumstance. My family has for generations farmed in the Ozark hills, and it was to that ancestral place of ours, now mine, that I retreated when the pandemic set the world awry. It is hard to write rationally about loss and all its sorrows surrounded by the ghosts of those you miss. The tethers holding you to reason and to training first draw taut, and then they fray, and finally they break. That at least is how it was for me.

I remember one day in particular from this time. Restless with self-disgust and guilt that I could not do my proper work, I wandered down to the barn, there to find some useful chore that I could make into an excuse for not doing what I ought. Instead, my then cursed mind lit upon an old yellow pencil, one of many that can litter up a place where one might need to make a mark on the way to building something sturdy. This one had great dents of teeth marks in it, from my uncle perhaps or my grandfather. One of them had closed his mouth tight round it and more than once – maybe in frustration or maybe just to hold it fast while hands were elsewhere busy. Just then I thought maybe I could write my book if I just used this pencil for my tool. When I cannot find just what I need, I will then add my teeth to his. I can gnarl it up, lay my damage onto his until the pencil finally breaks. But then, I thought, what a waste of this fine pencil. It wants proper work, not what I'm about. It wants frustrations come from nature, not from all our artifice – to mark out, say, a measurement on knotty wood I mean to cut, not to make dull recitations of purported wisdoms I myself reject.

I am not the sort to deny the value of our intellects or of work performed on paper for the benefit of the mind. I figure all have need of both mind and body, but for me at least writing up more staid philosophy for scholars would carry me just that step too far away from a world I want to keep. It is important, I still think, to study what wisdoms we human beings have managed hard to muster. But it also matters that we see when they won't do, that we hammer them hard upon the anvil of experience and let the ones that will just shatter. It doesn't matter what we write that up with, just that we make record of it. So that is what I did. To be clear, I don't here pretend I broke the wisdoms, only that I roughed them up a bit. I quit trying to sound smart and just said what I'm really saying. That is why I am finding this – my introduction to this book – so difficult to write.

I am here meant to tell what this book is about, to re-engage, to the satisfaction of a press and publisher, the organized mind that once hid my Grandpa's boots in a dense tome on moral theory. This, I should dutifully tell you, is a book that lights on themes important. I do talk about death and loss. Because of how these register for me, I also talk about a life in halves – a life in academia wrestling with ideas and a life in farming wrestling with land the way my ancestors also did. I talk about class and education, and how both can sometimes want to part you from your people. And I talk about philosophy and how I can't always make it do what I would like, though I never do resolve if that fault lies inside of it or me. These are the themes I should flag up for your notice. But if I say things in the way that I would mean them, I'd say that, because of how it came about, this is a book really about nothing and, in that way, perhaps about everything and all at once. It is most of all a refusal, at long belated last, of a mind that would keep the boots out.

2

What a Fellowship

Nick rises to an incomplete, hunched stand from where he has been crouching on the ground. He looks stiffly round the shop, hands on his knees, the shop floor now littered with tools and bits we thought might just prove useful. "I need . . . ," he pauses. "I need . . . a new body." We both laugh. He's a decade younger than me but far harder worn, some gaps where I still keep teeth, and hands much more long-battered than my own. I feel like we are friends, though we just met today and are the acquaintances of but a few hours. Perhaps it's the loneliness of the pandemic that does this. Or perhaps it's just that bonds will form where two people try together to solve a problem neither are well equipped to manage. Or perhaps it's just that we could both be counted sad.

Nick turned up at our farm early this morning when his truck broke down and he limped it into our lane to get it out of the dirt road. The trouble is the driveshaft, the failure of a patched-up job with bolts he did on it the first time that it failed. I wasn't home when he arrived, so both my father and daughter talked to him first. He'd asked if we had bolts, but they had told him no. They neither of them know their way around the shop or barns and both were wary of a stranger who looked rough. He had told both that he'd just wait there in his truck and call his mother to come get him. Both texted me to tell of him, so I made haste and went to talk to him. My husband was away so I was the best we had out here just now, for all that might be strange or challenging.

All apologies for breaking down in our lane, Nick explained the trouble in language I could only partly follow, for I was occupied with that assessment one must do out here with strangers. So few ever travel down our gravel road that one does not expect a stranger. Most out here are either known by us or can become so through a few short words of genealogy. Some of our people will know some of theirs, they'll be relatives of the people on that place out past where the creek regularly floods the road, or it turns out their second cousin was in school with my uncle way back when. Genuine strangers are rare and, because of this, a source of some trepidation. We are not on the way to anywhere a person with no near ties or kin would go, so one wonders at a stranger, the possibilities unlikely to console. I was reassured that our stranger seemed to know this, acting by the unspoken code for such circumstances by staying seated in his truck, not coming out to speak with me, not so much as putting a foot on our ground to stretch his legs. And he had a happy, well-kept dog with him, so there was that in testimony to his character as well.

Impatient with my uncertainties and, really, with it all – with the fear and wariness so long upon us all for this year of crouching low in melancholy seclusion – I told Nick, whose name I had just learned, to come on down to the shop. Down there I have sufficient bolts to secure the world entire, could I but locate where the loose joints are, so surely he could find the bits to make this little bit of broken world work more like the way it ought. So, too, I idly thought, he'd likely be out of here more quickly if he could just rig his truck rather than wait on a mother many miles from here, one so far disinclined, it seemed, to come. He did fix the truck, but it was not quick.

I directed Nick to coast the truck to the concrete pad that sits in front of the shop so that getting under it would involve less dirt and fewer ticks. Once settled there, we commenced a tour of the shop and milk barn in search of proper bolts, tools, and what else at all might be of aid.

The search for bolts of proper size and heft took the first half hour. That sounds a long time but owes to my grandfather's genius for thrift as it combined with his still opaque-to-me method of organization. He kept anything at all that might prove useful, and this included lots of bolts, but he never had the time or will to organize the too many useful bits he kept. There are handmade, stout oak drawers slid into one of the shelves, each filled entire with bolts and nuts. There are coffee cans of more, some stowed in old toolboxes that long ago lost their proper lids, and more as well inside the old wheel hub that serves as anchor to one of our sturdy clamps. And, too, over all the bolts and nuts sit walnuts stored by squirrels, nests made by mice, and stray bits of metal with functions yet to be determined. Our search for proper bolts began in concentration but soon turned toward other matters – mostly to a quest for this, quickly succeeded by a quest for that.

I won't here rehearse the wonder of it all. Let it suffice to say that by the time Nick's truck was running, we had dragged out some three different drills, half a dozen sets of bits, and several of the drill keys we'd had to try before we found one to fit. We'd unearthed the welding gear, though we decided against welding when after long searching we failed to find a single rod and, in ensuing consolation for this disappointment, admitted to each other that welders with no experience likely ought not learn on a truck aimed for the highway. Wrenches and sockets by the dozen littered the floor, neither of us being good at eyeballing bolts for size. Two heavy rubber gloves, now bereft of their cuffs, lay like dead hands on the workbench. We'd needed something to make up a gap between the shaft and its housing, and rubber glove cuffs, along with a bit of cork scavenged from the highest shelf, just did the trick. I can recite this, and still more I'll spare, about the leavings of our work because it would be days before I got it all put back in order. Every time I'd make a start, it seemed too melancholy a chore just then, the way that cleaning up after a party might be for those who like such things.

After about the first hour, our talk of needed tools and strategies to fix the truck gave way to other matters. We talked of Nick's dog Blue, who idled near the barn to sniff out rabbits while the work went on. Blue saved Nick's life, he said – although not in the tedious way of dogs like Lassie, as if Nick had fallen down a well. Unless of course, like me, you count the human condition itself too often like a well dug deep. Before Blue, Nick had two good dogs he'd counted as his heart, the sort of dogs that can keep one alive when life's other tethers thin to breaking. But then those dogs had passed and, left alone, Nick met with other troubles that made him want to die, troubles Blue couldn't solve but over which she could and did provide protecting salve.

Nick had spent time in jail, both in Springfield and in Poplar Bluff – the food, he said, much better at the first than at the second. His multiple crimes – at least those of which he spoke – are just that thing that often sends the poor to jail, the local paper's crime page a recitation of all the "failures to appear." With a warrant out for this, a traffic stop can quickly turn to jail, and so it was for Nick, and more than once. The phenomenon seems but a modern sort of debtor's prison, I could almost think.

Before coming back to our county to live with kin, Nick and Blue lived in a tent for two years over in Springfield, in a scrap of woods there. This bit of history made me see his being out by us as a fact no longer needing explanation. He'd early asked about a nearby conservation area, and I inferred he hoped that he might settle there and was on a jaunt to scope it out. His home life was the sort one has without a proper home.

He lately stayed some with cousins, though most times with his mother. She's an alcoholic, a fact she will confess when drunk but not while sober. She goes into the bathroom for long stretches, there to drink and cry, emerging swollen faced to say she should get treatment. By morning, she forgets all this again so nothing changes, a fact to wear upon the soul of a good son. In truth, I don't know if Nick is a good son or not, or even what that means in a family like his.

The broke-down truck outside our shop is new to Nick. He had a better one, he said, but one his own aunt had stolen. Some several months ago, he'd parked it on the street beside her house and, when it disappeared, she claimed the county came and took it. But the county had no record, and the manner of his aunt in this false telling told Nick all he thought he ought to know. He'd had nothing but a bicycle for months, each trip out a devil's choice: stay isolated out on the rural highway where his mother lives or bike the many miles to get to town. The highway where his mother lives is one familiar to me, though I have never there seen one mad or desperate enough to take it on by bike. The pavement drops away to brush and wilds, with no margin for the some extra that a bike alongside trucks and cars would take. It's a pleasure in a truck, the hills all rolling out, some steep enough to send a stomach in a plummet if you take them nicely fast enough. But those hills are not the stuff for bikes or if they are, they'd be for those who bike in helmets and tight pants, masochistic sportsmen who welcome hurt, not people with no other transportation and enough hurt not to volunteer for more.

Nick said he mostly stayed away from town. Said that by the time he could even get himself to Dollar General, the store closest to his mother's place, he'd be so worn down by biking that none of what it offered could any longer tempt. He could not stay away entirely, for he's in the care of the local mental health clinic and must attend his appointments. That clinic is another two miles in, though at least the streets by then have largely leveled off. Nick said he mostly sought there for reasons he should keep on living, but the pills the doctors gave him hadn't yet provided reasons or even offered up a better way to look for some. He mostly didn't fuss with them, he said, though he continued on biweekly with his visits, visits he had hoped could be improved upon if he could drive instead of bike. All of this is but to say that Nick's truck was meant to be the most ambitious sort of blessing, the kind that changes life entire.

Nick's new truck is a beater, bought from a guy who was taking it to the salvage yard to sell for bail money for a cousin. Nick used all his savings, some $400, and took it off the guy. He'd already rigged that driveshaft once, though he had then owned it only for three days. The rigging job he'd made was not the best, so we sought throughout to do better, our hopes pinned on the cork and rubber glove combination as a bid to make a better fit, something to keep the bolts from shearing off with the vibrations as he drove.

With a truck that mostly worked, he might gain back his profession, get a "real job," and escape sometimes his drunk and weeping mother. Nick is a hairdresser by trade, certified, he said, by one of those familiar names that show up on shampoo – Vidal Sassoon? Paul Mitchell? I can't now recall. I don't know what took him out of his profession, whether it was the jail time, the homelessness, or the depression. He still cut hair when he could, but this was not often since it must be done from home, and never brought in much. I assume that's how he accumulated the savings he'd invested in the truck.

Throughout this recitation of his life, I mostly only listened. Sometimes I think we mainly need someone to marvel with us at life's woes – not one to carry on or pitch to solve them, but one who can just say and mean it: Damn, that's hard. So that's about all I had to say. This might suggest the conversation was one-sided, but I would never call it so. Just as he'd reached some new height of sorrow, Nick would coast back down with the laughing style of freedom that comes with telling up so one can shuffle off the worst. "So," he'd say, "that's what my mother is like – how's yours?" Or, "Well, now you know my whole life story, so tell me yours as well." The only bit I found uneasy in it all came when he became self-conscious about the hours we were spending and the need for my hands on the task as well as his. He would then say that he was sure I had better or more important or more fun things to be doing than this. Or he'd ask what my real plan for this day had been. I did not want to say.

How does one go about saying that one had planned to spend the day writing a book about death? It seems such a breathtakingly stupid thing to try to do and one easily traded for a broken driveshaft. Both are problems I know not at all how to solve, but only one has good company and conversation. Better, clearly, to learn about the mashed potatoes in the Springfield jail, to admire, out loud and together, the singular consolations of a good dog, to triumph in that last drill bit, the only one that refused to break – to speak, ultimately, in all our wild loneliness while we solved this one trouble among all the stubborn rest.

In truth, my will for what I call my work is weak. My job title is all fancy – I am Professor of Philosophy – but really, there are too many times I find it but an embarrassment to be a philosopher. One day, when I'd been doing outdoor work that made one filthy, my uncle marveled out loud at me and said something I've long struggled to forget. Retired, and joyful with it, he said, "You know, I worked all my life so I could at last just sit down to read and think." The implication is the too familiar curiosity of my job to most out here: I get *paid* to sit and read and think. Too often, I don't really want to do those things. I also tire of being the stone in an otherwise fine pot of rice, the bit of buckshot cooked into the meat, the stuff to crack a conversation's tooth. Owning up to being a philosopher, to being what I sometimes have to be, is an ending.

My other uncle – the one most sparing with his words – sometimes used to remark to me that I should beware because my "brains were showing." Most often this was because I'd interjected knowledge when idle speculation was all a conversation needed. Sometimes when people pose a question, an answer isn't really what is wanted. Instead, the question is a sort of summons, an invitation to all around to speculate and wonder. The one who speaks an answer definite has missed the point entire. And so I sometimes did. Then Bob would wryly grin and alert me to my indiscretion. It would come in a soft aside, the way you tell someone their underpants are showing so that they can fix them before all around take notice. Brains are not a problem. You just need to know when and how to use them. Like underpants, they make you fit for human company but are not a thing to put upon display.

I here drift into all I thought but did not say to Nick. Being a philosopher, for me, amounts to never wanting to own up out loud to what you are or should be doing. There's just no good way to tell a man in sorrow that were it not for his broken driveshaft, I'd be thinking about death. So I just don't. We talk instead about my hair.

Nick offers to give me a haircut, both in payment for my labor and tools, as well, he says, in friendship. I take his number just in case I someday want a haircut, but I think it is unlikely. The last time I had my hair cut by someone else was decades ago and for my wedding, a history I tell to Nick. He cuts his own as well, so he is not dismayed. We compare our current hairdos, both adorned with dust where we have lain beneath the truck, both shaggy with sweat and work. We conclude together that we look fine, just as we are. We compliment each other's mess of hair and together laugh to find ourselves so satisfied with how we look. But all the same, Nick does allow, it is a good that people don't know that they can cut their own hair and will pay someone to do it. "You gotta find something someone will pay you to do," he says. Maybe it's not terrible after all that I get paid to think about death. So far at least, it pays, even if anyone can do it.

After more than four hours at it, Nick's driveshaft is fixed, at least enough so he can risk our highway, then his own. I send him off with peanut butter crackers and a Coke, a bone for Blue. My day is my own again, but I will not think of death just yet. I will think instead of chance. About my grandfather's bolts, lain by and furred with dust, gone now down the road, about how I hope they hold. Let fortune, just for this and just for now, be once kind.

3

Heat-Strengthened

I have been thinking about this book on death for years, been trying to write it now for more than four. Before the pandemic, I had laid a plan that charted out just how this book should go. I had outlines of the chapters, each neatly devised to address a particular aspect of bereavement. I had, too, a bibliography made dense by articles and texts representing both the latest and the most storied of philosophers who turned their attentions to addressing death. In the book, as already in its outline, I would take on my other voice, that one I'm paid to use, the one with patience well employed to outline arguments, "show my work," and develop firm conclusions. It was to be the kind of book that other philosophers would read, what we who study and do research would call a "contribution to the literature." But I have grown too restive for that voice. My complaints about what it is to be an academic philosopher are many, and most involve what I have come to see as the distortions of my natural character that the profession has performed upon me.

I have lately been reading a book, *An Immense World*, about animal perception. In it, the author Ed Yong details the radical variety of ways of perceiving the world. In some important sense, an animal's sensory capacities distill the stuff of experience into just those features that it can register. Creatures notice only what their senses are built to notice: The dog's world is a cornucopia of odors, the spider's is focused on vibrations, the tick's world is a place of scent and heat. Following the early twentieth-century biologist Jakob von Uexkull, Yong calls a world so distilled an *Umwelt,* and every species has its own, an experienced environment shaped by what it is capable of noticing. Our senses do not tell us what the world is like; they tell us only the bits of it that we are biologically equipped to recognize. In this, we all are limited. Or, as that old biologist Uexkull says, the world writ large is "constricted and transformed into an impoverished structure" dictated by the needs and capacities of the creature who experiences it.

I am tempted by Yong's work to make a fanciful study of my own, to treat the contemporary academic philosopher as its own species with its own distinctive *Umwelt.* As Yong observes, no creature can afford to attend to all within its environs, and the senses of each are built for selectivity, for noticing just those features of environment that it somehow pays to notice – those that conduce to avoiding threats, finding nourishment, and, most generally, to surviving. I cannot here assay what complex evolutionary pressures have produced the *Umwelt* of the philosopher, but it suits me to think of philosophers as not unlike the common tick. A tick is built for finding blood, turning its heightened olfactory powers and heat detection toward this effort. A philosopher is built for argument, for seeking out reasons and justification, for abstract thinking and conceptual complexity. Both naturally miss out on other sorts and styles of experience. But for both, survival may depend upon the operation of our special focus.

Contemporary philosophy, like many academic disciplines, presently operates under the horrifying dictum *publish or perish.* That is, if one will get and keep a job, one must produce research. Like most creatures, philosophers prefer survival. So, they produce and publish. Ordinary people will likely not have encountered any of the resulting flood of published philosophy, for it is placed in specialized academic journals and with academic presses, its audience the other ticks. It operates within an *Umwelt* that other creatures – which is to say, other people – largely do not share. Philosophical perception is specially narrowed to meet the survival and success conditions of the profession as it presently functions in contemporary academia. What journals and presses will publish is what we must adjust ourselves to seeing and to saying. You need senses well adapted and constrained to endure the world of our profession.

Philosophical success, and thus philosophical perception, is driven by argumentation, but argumentation of a specially constricted sort. A generally strong argument will give someone reasons to accept a conclusion or, more modestly, to consider the conclusion plausible and worthy of careful consideration. But the contemporary philosopher's version of argumentation goes well beyond the generally strong. It aspires to be unassailable, to armor the one who offers it against any and all objections. A host of peculiarities and idiosyncrasies follow from this most basic aspiration, but let me just describe the psychology of it all, at least as I experience it.

It turns out that there are very few philosophical conclusions one might draw that cannot be assailed. However, one reliable strategy to minimize objections is to keep conclusions modest – smaller targets are easier to guard than larger ones. Gone are the days when philosophers wildly speculated or ruminated ambitiously about thoughts still incomplete or half-formed. Instead, one should seek to offer only what one can defend, and defend under the heavy assault of eager critics, and it won't just be one's conclusion that they're after. Precision in language – in how one's terms are defined and employed, in how one articulates one's reasons and the relations between them – is crucially important. Vagueness is a vice; rigor our cardinal virtue. Even a relatively good argument will have neighboring arguments that are bad, so one must take care to distinguish, with quasi-scientific exactitude, what one is offering from any nearby lesser possibilities. One will need to eschew any ambiguities. Enlivening thinking practices, such as the appeal to analogy or employment of metaphor, are undertaken only at one's risk. Above all, one should entertain and convincingly answer any objections that one's view could possibly invite. One will not succeed in this, for no one could, but still and all, one should give a mighty effort at it.

All of what I here describe may well sound paranoid, a style of thinking undertaken in a defensive crouch because enemies are everywhere. But, as the saying goes, it's not paranoid if they really are after you. The contemporary philosopher's *Umwelt* is a place of danger because philosophical reasoning is so tightly tethered to philosophical critique. The surest test of whether an argument is any good, so the reasoning would go, is whether it can withstand concentrated opposition. Both in print and in person, philosophers habitually engage each other in such opposition, their interactions dominated by conversational spirals of objection and reply. This naturally creates a feedback loop. Accustomed to having one's ideas assailed by others, one tries better to armor them. But still the critics come. So one tries to armor them some more or shrink the target smaller still. The senses become at once narrowed and acutely tuned to perils. Readers more accustomed to metaphorical language than philosophers tend to be may have noticed that my language has taken on some rather martial atmospherics. I have slid away from ticks and into something else entire. This is because I cannot help myself because, alas, I am too thoroughly a tick for my own good.

Contemporary philosophers habitually describe their own *Umwelt* in language evocative of fighting and of war. This is how we see and represent among ourselves the nature of the world that we experience. We use the language of "attack" to describe the ways we treat each other's work. Argument is "combat," philosophers "gunslingers." To engage in debate with ordinary people is, for a philosopher, like bringing a gun to a knife fight – quickly over and with much one-sided verbal bloodshed. Even other academics find us sometimes nigh intolerable, a fact boastingly acknowledged by one philosopher who noted that our aggressive style "would be considered unseemly in other disciplines." In my own modest midwestern department, after we subject visiting speakers to vigorous question-and-answer sessions, some of my colleagues express great satisfaction that while we might be small, still we "punch above our weight class." The implications are here so weird that I must trace them out. In the *Umwelt* of philosophers, a guest left bloodied by a punching host is counted a success all round. The guest can come away knowing just where her soft spots are so she can later guard them better, and the host has further honed the pugilistic skills that can conduce to his own survival. (One can build an entire career in contemporary philosophy simply publishing papers that articulate the small errors of others or offer minor corrections to minor points made by one's fellows on their own way to their own minor conclusions.) The language philosophers use to describe our world is of course a lot of macho posturing and foolishness, but let me just indulge the point and take it all the way it goes for me.

In addition to reading about animal perception, I have lately been reading English history too, and was last night captivated by one death that stood out for me amidst the many bloody battles. In his *War of the Roses*, Dan Brown describes the conditions under which the war was fought and the armor that the best would wear. Atop an underlayer of fabric would be sewn chain mail, the mail close fitted and the thread for the sewing the stoutest then available. Over this would go "heat-strengthened and highly polished metal," the armor itself, encompassing all "from throat to toe." Lest we forget the head, this would bear the helmet, along with its visor equipped with but a "tiny slit through which to view the terror of the slaughter." Of course, wearing all this gear presents a hazard of its own. An armored knight knocked to the ground will struggle against all that weighty metal to try to rise again. But what most caught my attention is a poor fellow named John, Lord Clifford. At twenty-five, he had already survived multiple conflicts. On the day of his death, having violently captured a contested bridge, he removed his neck guard to take a drink. And that is when an arrow ran him through the throat. In fifteenth-century war, you must wear gear that forbids relieving thirst. What sight of things you might achieve will be glimpsed through an altogether narrow slit, an *Umwelt* made too small and by the choice to don that armor. Both human perception and human need are sacrificed for raw survival. This is how philosophy has come to feel to me. I, too, could use a drink.

I should not here belabor all this business about how professional philosophy is currently constrained and so constraining, far less continue to mix talk of ticks and Lancastrian nobles. If I am honest, and by now I surely should be, my principal motivation is defensiveness. I seek to explain a waste of mortal hours, how I could for several years pursue an idea that I have, far too belatedly, come to judge as terrible and more than a little ridiculous.

The book that I was going to write had a conclusion made most definite. I was going to show that bereavement is, and perhaps can only be, confusion. I was going to *argue* for confusion, and then defend it against all comers. I would consider other arguments, the ones that aspire to establish something better than confusion as to what we can make of death, but mostly to expose their weak spots and then to dispatch them. Worse still, in my work on this, I attempted a precise taxonomy of confusions – all the different kinds that come in grief and from what sources each may come. This naturally entailed that I exercise great effort at precision and at rigor – if you will make a *system* of confusions, you will need to carefully distinguish each from each. Finally, and at long last, I understood the gruesome folly of it all. Somehow, in the course of my own rich and varied life, I came to start a book about how grief appears glimpsed through a helmet slit.

My conclusion about the experiences come in bereavement has not changed. Really, the best thing I can say of these is that they are all confusion. But I will no longer try to argue that. I do not think it can be done. Genuine confusion, I expect, is much like genuine humility – it is not a thing well captured by one come in the full armor of reasoning and intellect. It is not a thing to assert or defend – if you must defend your own humility, you likely do not have it, and so it is with confusion. If it can be laid out in exacting, precise language, it has become something altogether different, a bloodless abstraction never met yet in life. Even if it could be done, if a rigorous argument for confusion could be made, I am no longer one to make it.

4

Some Glad Morning

My people have been farmers for several generations, our family's homeplace a couple of hundred acres of pasture and woods in the southern Missouri Ozarks. The year my grandfather Lynn died, 2013, was the farm's one-hundredth year. Family farms in the Ozarks rarely last a century, a fact sometimes told boastingly upon the ones that do. These have signs the state of Missouri will award upon request, signs proclaiming the place a "Century Farm," the status given farms when a family has managed, against the odds, to hold it long enough to qualify. Far more common are farms that, however long they managed in the end, the families that held them finally lost.

The region around our farm is a lacework of gravel roads that trace through hill country, and what happens when families like ours just can't keep it all going is told everywhere upon these roads. Abandoned farmhouses sit in fields given over to elaborate beef cattle operations held by wealthy ranchers who buy up old places when a family can no longer keep them. In these places, the fencing is bright and taut, well maintained but by people who live elsewhere. The tarpaper and rock homes that once sheltered families working the land become just bits of a landscape, too much trouble to tear down when the elements will eventually do the work for you. Some old homeplaces don't even have the care of wealthy ranchers but instead sit nested in trees that have come up since the families left, the houses now effectively forested. Bereft of the people who kept the houses whole, they become home to all manner of wildlife, though given the area, some also come to host meth cookers. But the most haunted examples, I find, are the old family farms where no house at all still sits. On spring's arrival, they emerge like ghosts across the landscape, as vast armies of yellow daffodils arise to tell of what once was. The daffodils stand in fragile, temporary signal, their patterns marking out where a house once stood – now lining a path where no path sits or surrounding where a porch once stood. The daffodils stubbornly outlast the ones who planted them and abide as the only sign of what was once a homeplace.

I had always found a wild melancholy beauty in the wrecks of farms that populate the region. Human beings are hopeful, tragic sorts of things. They work and build, struggle and strive, yet nature will assert herself. For when we stop our work, she comes in force to reclaim quickly what was hers. A house stout built by eager hands will yield, as all things must, before the onslaught of untended time. What humans build will bloom then fade and at last vanish, and something of the fineness of it all comes from the fact its fineness cannot last. But then I discovered that the pleasingly melancholy aesthetics of decay are only lovely at a distance. Transience can be exquisite, but only when it is that of others. When it's your own, it's mostly just a horror.

Of all my grandparents left behind, the farm was root to every branch, our family's history worked into the ground itself. The cistern of my great-great grandmother's house, all that's left of her own homeplace, lay hidden under brush along one hillside. Virginia creeper that my great-grandmother Della planted still climbed the barn walls. The bent tree where my grandfather sat as a boy to fish stood yet along the creek.

The ruins of a cabin my uncle built when he was young were nestled on a wooded hill. My mind could readily make recitations such as this, rehearsals of the place and all it so distinctly held. But then, I would imagine, such recitations too are but the standard way. Out among the ghostly daffodils are stories just like this – those flowers signal places someone counted specially theirs and believed to be exceptions to the common doom.

My grandfather's will left the farm entire to his three children, Bob, Don, and my mother, the eldest, Kay. They each would keep some small acreage, but none could keep the farm entire. The heart of it, more than a couple hundred acres, would go to auction, and without that heart, the rest was bound to follow. A monied rancher would first surround then surely swallow all, and my mother's generation would likely be our last upon that place. That's when we, my husband and I, academics both, decided that the troubles induced by grief would not be shuffled off but parceled out, just like our brand new home-equity loan, across what years remained to us. We bought the farm. We lodged our fates inside its history, though its history was, just then, a tale of some decline.

Over its century, the farm had included pigs, chickens, and goats, but its most successful years, my grandfather's prime working years, were devoted to dairy cattle, Holsteins whose gentle nature could lull one into the complacent belief that cattle are inherently docile and tamely compliant. My grandfather died at 95 but had retired some ten years earlier. The years that followed his retreat from the day-to-day workings of the farm were its most troubled, but the seeds of the farm's decline were planted earlier still. A family dairy needs both many hands and the income to sustain them all, a fragile balance that for our family tipped, then tipped again.

In the farm's best years, my grandfather and my uncles worked the place together. They never made a lot of course, but then they couldn't make enough. Milk prices cratered in the 1980s. Then the hay barn burned, along with all that would have fed the stock through winter, and the balance then first tipped. Since the farm could not sustain them all, Don and his family left to seek work elsewhere. The farm would then be worked by Grandpa and Bob, two carrying on as three once did. When Grandpa at last retired under the combined pressures of aging and arthritis, the balance tipped again, leaving only one to carry on as two had, and this, finally, culminated in the end of the dairy.

In the half dozen years or so before my grandfather's death, Bob earned income by leasing pasture to a wealthy rancher whose rent cows – this is what we called them – were a trial upon the land. These were no mild-mannered Holsteins accustomed to the daily interactions of milking, but beef cattle that, for want of human contact, were by unpredictable turns spooky and aggressive. With the pastures unmanaged and the rancher inattentive, the rent cows overgrazed the land and when they had done their worst on one field, would crash through weak fencing in search of another. During these years, Bob also secured income by selling off equipment idled when the dairy stopped. The milk tank went, as did, finally, any bits of metal he could scare up to sell for scrap. Bob tried, in short, to keep things going in the ways he found to hand, but eventually this amounted to little more than trying to turn whatever could be turned into money sufficient for bare living. The frustrations and sorrows of this explain why, upon my grandfather's death, Bob himself wanted none of the farm but his own house and a small patch of pasture.

Our purchase of the farm finalized in spring, so we continued with our classes and laid plans in leisure for when summer would release us to that work. The rent cows were gone so we hoped the pastures would recover, but we would surely need to patch some fences, maybe clear what brush had grown where none should be. Chores like these, and others we might find, could come as we learned the lay of things and planned what we might do. This is how we thought, before we found the great and gaping space between what one expects and what one finds.

In 2013, the entire county was under siege by musk thistle, an aggressive invasive species that destroys field fescue, the stuff for hay and grazing, and that left unchecked diabolically reproduces itself at a rate that beggars belief. At its worst, musk thistle stalks grow to seven or eight feet in height and in dense clusters that utterly overwhelm any undergrowing grass. The plant's initial blooms emerge as balls of beautifully delicate and thready purple. But from purple, the threads pale into white and, just like dandelion heads, each thread bears seed all too ready to cast off into the world to produce another thistle. Each thistle plant, I learned, can produce up to 20,000 seeds, and thus each represents the threat of 20,000 more. This malevolent talent for reproduction explains why the Environmental Protection Agency considers farms with uncontained thistle a hazard worthy of steep fines.

While every farm in our area had some thistle to contend with that summer, ours was utterly conquered and consumed, the fields impassable even for walking unless one wanted to scythe a way through dense thickets grown higher than oneself. Years of rent cows overgrazing unmanaged pastures had created the perfect conditions to make ours a farm where naught would grow but thistle, a place of utter pestilence. I remember acutely when I first took in the landscape. My memory has fixed that moment not because I found the horror that I ought have felt, but because I didn't. My ignorance now staggers me, but then I only vaguely thought the unbroken sea of purple stretched before me somewhat pretty. Even in this folly, I did also have the sense to think: I don't remember the farm ever looking quite like this before. In hindsight, it is likely a mercy that I failed to see the menace all at once and came instead to understand it slowly. Some things it's best not to know until you're in them and the chance for flight has passed.

The EPA did not come calling, but the neighbors surely did. Because this is the Ozarks, none were angry or too frank. Instead, they worked on us through indirection, come with congratulations that we kept the farm, felicitations always followed by a pregnant pause, then talk of thistle. For of course our thistle would not long be ours alone: Once its purple turned to white, the wind would gift our seed to all our neighbors. These conversations found their natural end because we were soon no longer free to talk. Within days, we had a tractor and a brushhog mower, along with the years of payments they required. From idle reveries about future plans, we swiftly settled on the only plan: cut down all the thistle.

Between the two of us, Garret and I kept the tractor mowing through all daylight hours for days that seemed unending. Words between us thinned to what would fit while trading shifts, the tractor left to idle while one climbed down and one climbed up. The work was slow, as if we cut each field by inches. So dense was all the thistle, we could only creep along, for one could neither cut well nor spy a blade-fouling rock at any rate of speed. But in this way we managed for a while, laying flat the acres inch by steady inch, till even this, our "plan," would also founder. The dust and fluff kicked up by all our mowing made a misery throughout, and Garret soon enough was plainly ill with it, ravaged by a sinus infection that left him feverish and felled. So I was left to soldier on alone. In my cutting without respite, I too developed something like a fever, though mine was of another order, as if a madness had set in.

A special form of insensibility can be achieved when one is trapped within a task impossible and repetitive, or so it was for me. I would think that I should think, there upon the tractor. Aware I was no farmer, I could at least stay a philosopher. But what thoughts might come were mostly plain and where they weren't, they were defeated. To lay flat the thistle was to see what it concealed. Thorn trees grew in clusters of fresh menace. Barbed-wire fencing stretched slack and sloppy where it was not breached and broken. Fenceposts hand cut from oak sometimes dangled in the wire, unmoored from the ground in which they ought to stand, hanging useless like mere ornaments.

My circuits of the fields took on a leaden rhythm. I felt doomed to make a never-ending journey of the place, laying waste to thistle just to see more waste I could not fix. One day I almost mowed a fawn newly birthed. It struggled to its feet just in time to dodge the blade. At least, I dully thought, I have not mowed down that fawn. Soon after this, I took to singing hymns of consolation at a shout. By then I knew no sound of mine would ever rise above the wails of all my cutting – the deep roar of tractor engine and slapping cracks of blade on thistle drown out all – and so I turned to sacrilege because I might as well. "Some glad morning when this life is o'er, I'll fly away," I would shriek and call. I doubted any morning could be bright since all mornings started but more cutting. Still, here was a truth worth keeping: I will at least one day be dead. Hallelujah by and by.

And then I found one last rent cow.

Before we took on the farm, Bob had ended the lease arrangement with the rancher whose cows had eaten the place bare. When the rancher collected his stock, however, there was one heifer he could not catch. So he just left her there, professing a vague plan to Bob to hire cowboys who might have more success in corralling her into a trailer. As with his cattle more generally, he was unconcerned about this last straggler, so she had been out among the thistle, starving and alone for weeks that then grew into months.

Cattle are of course herd animals and not meant to live alone, much less to live upon land where grazing is scarce and the combined effects of starvation and loneliness work upon the bovine mind to ill effect. Half mad in conditions not made for her sort, she had developed into the worst a cow can be, a thing of sadness hardened into unreasoning desperation. She and I developed a relationship. I tried several times to drive her forward toward the barn, toward an enclosure where I could keep and feed her, and our encounters made us both the worse for wear. She would sometimes flee me, sometimes charge me, but nothing I did could draw her in where I could keep her penned so her owner could be forced to come to collect her.

As the cow and I would career about the fields, her in panicked flight and me in clumsy pursuit, we made a fitting pair, two females of their species clinging to a world demonstrably not fitted to their own best interests. We'd crash through thistle and broken fencing, both rendered stupid at losing the protection of their herd. She wanted her cows, I wanted all of it and all of them, the farm as was and in hands beyond my weary, untrained own. Neither of us could have what we wanted, but at least for a time we had each other.

That poor rent cow was eventually caught, but it did take cowboys on horseback to do it. By the time they came, her deterioration was such that she would go from field to trailer to slaughter. I have at least enjoyed a better fate than this.

5

I Think, Maybe, It Isn't

My route into philosophy was more orthodox and gradual than my beginnings in farming. Even so, I can in hindsight see in it the seeds of my present discontent. In my first philosophy class, when I was but nineteen or so, we began with Parmenides. Parmenides is among those earliest of Greek philosophers, and only spare fragments of his work survive. My professor explained Parmenides' claim that "It is," a deceptively simple bit of language meant to indicate an entire view of reality. By Parmenides' reckoning, reality is a singular one, a unified totality, an "it" – a view philosophers would come to call monism. Understanding this, according to Parmenides, would constitute real knowledge, for it is only our fallible and mistaken senses that lead us to think the world a place of change, flux, and transformation.

It is hard for me to be certain now, but I think at nineteen I did understand the view Parmenides was after. However, I was not easy with it. I had been a high school dropout and then a college dropout, and was just then finding my way back to formal learning. I had never yet spoken out loud in any college class, but this business of Parmenides ruptured, finally, my silence. "How did he live?" I asked. My professor responded, with admirable patience but some confusion, that Parmenides taught, debated, and dialogued with other philosophers. I interrupted, "Yes, but how did he *live*?" The professor next made some remarks that showed his patience wearing thin, gesturing at all we do not know and the likelihood that Parmenides lived like any other Greek. I did not ask again, and soon learned that this is not really the sort of question well-suited to the academic study of philosophy.

When I first began at it, I expected that philosophy should *do* something to you, that if you labor after ideas, those ideas should, somehow, make an alteration – whether that be to help one thrive, to endure life's travails, to see and understand more, or even just to appreciate our mortal human limits and develop some sense about where and what those are. I wanted Parmenides to have some mode and manner of life vouchsafed by "It is." I wanted to know what thinking this *did to him*. Not much, I gather, but that's about what I suspected. His did not seem to be a view that could change much, given that it denied the reality of change itself. Even so, back then I had the naive sense that once a philosopher arrived at his conclusion – his Big Idea, so to speak – that would then govern all for him, transform his life into whatever wisdom is. Even as I have stayed with philosophy for years and never asked it again out loud, the question stuck around. How does one *live*? Now that my days as an academic philosopher are numbered, I have come back to ask it one last time.

Asking how a philosopher will live is asking about many things, and many things at once. One is asking, implicitly, about the power of ideas, about the will of one who seeks to wield them, about the nature of any contact between life and the sense we seek to make of it. As I asked it at nineteen, the question presupposed that there is something kin to wisdom that can make one different than the rest. Many of the ancients looked for this, or something like. From the Hellenistic Epicureans and Stoics to the Indian Vedic philosophers to the early Chinese Daoists and then to Buddhists of all sorts, philosophers sought ways to make a life that might better suit the one who lives it. All different in their particulars and the Big Ideas that they offer, all nonetheless promise their practitioners ways to tame and calm the upheavals of experience. One need not live as others do, hurled chaotically about by events that set one's emotions and psychology careening. Wisdom that comes through study, practice, and reflection can confer the peace that so much of life would deny us. The models of this differ – some would have us lodging in a mental still point set apart from the roiling storms of experience, while others recommend the flex to flow along with whatever waves of change arise. Yet for all, the turmoil of emotions that beset others does not afflict the wise. Experience is tamed by insight, the wise guarded by the Big Idea. This was what many of the ancients promised, but few philosophers openly seek it now.

Contemporary philosophy has largely given up the hunt for Big Ideas of the sort the ancients sought. As human knowledge has increased, the scope of philosophy has contracted. Philosophy long ago gave up to the sciences, both natural and social, a lot of what it once addressed, and this is largely for the better. (It is far more useful to consult a biologist than Aristotle if you want to understand animals or, for that matter, women.) As our subject matter has contracted, so too have our methods and techniques, and the results that we expect. Rather than hunt for the Big Idea, or even wisdom, we seek lesser forms of sense – that is, to make some sense of a world now carved into far smaller pieces. Progress in this style is marked in small increments, and there is good that can be said of this. At least, we philosophers now see more of just how vexing a place the world can be. Rather than sum it up with any Big Idea, we chip away at it and do not try to tame it all at once. How do philosophers who practice philosophy in this way *live*? This is a question I can answer well enough since I have been one.

There is of course an entire specialized domain of human inquiry, sociology, devoted to assessing how particular human populations live, so if we want a reliable and informed account of the philosophers, we'd have to ask a sociologist. But if I wanted to answer the question in the spirit that I asked it at nineteen, I think I'd tell my younger self that the philosophers nowadays live akin to those who are passionate scrapbookers. Hobby and craft stores feature aisle upon aisle of material for creating fantastically elaborate scrapbooks. No more sticking your family photographs into a shoebox or gluing them onto stiff paper pages in a dime-store photo book. Now there are special papers, stickers, labels, stamps, and all manner of embellishments. Avid scrapbookers can produce a family record of events bearing excruciatingly detailed decoration and flourish, each page distinct in theme or motif, each a collage of different colors, scripts, and textures. Of course, even the most avid scrapbooker isn't always at it. They pursue their passion alongside all the rest of life, making meals, running errands, or idling on the couch. So it is for philosophers.

All human beings have and value both memory and reason. Some just take this having and valuing well past what is usual. Scrapbookers turn memory into a special project; philosophers do the same with reason. Both can naturally be obnoxious with it, as, say, when a scrapbooker eyes a present, living scene for how she might turn it to account upon a page or when a philosopher can't enjoy a casual banter because he's too busy unearthing and announcing banter's unstated premises. Such is to say that for both, the passion and its special preoccupations may overtake one's capacity to enjoy other of life's goods. Both also share a kind of taming impulse. Both seek to lend an uncommon order to things, to what we want to keep in recollection or what we want to understand. And both construct the order that they seek in quite small increments, the scrapbooker capturing life page by slow page, the contemporary philosopher "contributing to the literature" likewise.

Like a scrapbooker, a contemporary philosopher lives with a devotion to something broad and general in a way that is quite specific and intricate, even perhaps baroque. And, for the most part, the wider contours of life beyond this devotion go on for him as they go on for others. This at least is how I have come to think of my profession. It has settled into something less like questing after wisdom and more like a reliably rational, if sometimes neurotic, routine for making small sense.

Of these modes of philosophy, the ancient and the new, I am most tempted by the ancient. But I have grown skeptical of an impulse that they in common share, the impulse to tame and order. I oppose neither wisdom nor the more modest effort to make some sense. Yet my only Big Idea is that there is, for me at least, no Big Idea that makes an alteration, no singular way to tame the biggest troubles. My own smaller form of progress making sense amounts to knowing when some sense cannot be made or, put more precisely, when the effort to divide a problem into smallest parts will miss the problem altogether.

The most striking element in philosophy that speaks to bereavement, and the one I count most useless, is that it is written mostly by those for whom the mess of loss has passed, if mess it ever was for them. It operates at best in a kind of retrospective, with all the aching turmoil now dissipated into order. Any confusions or agonies that might appear pose but as problems described because a "solution" will be soon delivered. The philosophers who write on loss do so mostly when they have an answer in the offing. Philosophy about loss is not unique in this – philosophy gets written when, and seemingly only when, the philosopher has *worked things out,* when the problem has been tamed. To find philosophers visibly uneasy in their sorrows, you have to look where biography can rupture up the "wisdom" – to Confucius, say, cursing heaven and collapsing into weeping when his beloved, best student dies; to Zhuangzi interrupting all his clever insight to cry over his dead wife; to Lucretius seeming just to lose his mind as he describes the horrors of a plague; to Montaigne melancholically aching for a friend, Cicero for a daughter, Seneca briefly for a friend. These are the bits of the philosophers that I most like, but they don't much pass for what we lately call "philosophy," if they ever did. They rarely receive any notice, but if they do, they're taken as but some fragmentary chaos, oddities one passes on the way to cleaner wisdoms, that tidy stuff that offers up some hope that we have worked things out.

Seeking to wrest sense from confusion is, as a general matter, a human art we rightly prize. It is helpful and important to tame the wilds, to map ways to pass through danger, to chart with reason ways to not get lost. Yet clarity and answers can also be a kind of vice. This happens when our answers are too facile or too fluid. It happens when our answers are abstruse, lifted out into abstractions not enough like life, or intricate in arcane mental "moves" that the stiff joints of real experience cannot make. These are vices well attested and often recognized, even by we who likely make them most. But another sort might be more basic still, trying to solve what maybe we cannot. Or, perhaps more exactly still, it might be the case that the richest of confusions are things to live alongside, not to solve.

During the first year and a half of the pandemic, I lived on my farm, helping out my parents, teaching my students online, and retreating to the woods when I needed most just to escape. In all of this, I was joined by a stray dog who had some years prior been dumped at a homeplace up the way. For reasons only he would know, he took me up as his. Dog – for so a neighbor named him and in a way that stuck – became my nearest companion for weeks stretched into months and then well out beyond a year. When I was outdoors, he was always with me; when I was indoors, he waited sentry on the porch. Some mix of Great Pyrenees and a bit of Saint Bernard, Dog was an enormous creature. He was a companion of an order I have never found before, nor am I like to do again – he, my shadow and protector, my familiar and my sometime muse.

But despite our long acquaintance and companionship, he was also always, and ever would be, a creature of the wild. As my husband aptly put it, it was as if I had been befriended by a wolf. For a dog that has lived by its wits as long as Dog had by then done is not a one that may be tamed.

However mild Dog might sometimes pose or even be, the feral never left him. I saw him kill armadillos, beavers, rabbits, groundhogs, and, once, a grown coyote. In case it is not clear, a dog that can kill a coyote is a fearsome wonder of a beast – one who has not just an uncommon potency of jaw and muscle but instinct and courage to inspire awe. What such a dog is not, however, is a creature one can make entirely one's own. You may befriend and keep company, but to domesticate him, if indeed it could be done, would be to betray some ineluctable brute, raw beauty that is his. More to the point, should you somehow come to think you'd pulled this off, you would almost certainly be wrong, and perhaps dangerously so. The wild can be subdued for a time, but wild will out.

In the pandemic months I spent with Dog, I could not do philosophy. Life entire seemed to have gone wild. So I did instead whatever else was near to hand, and that mostly amounted to retreating for long hours in the woods with Dog. I have never yet drawn any firm conclusions from this time, but I have come to suspect that some of what is best in thinking, and in living, comes not out of but inside a fundamental chaos, when you give up forcing things to take a shape and let them be just as they are. Not all that is wild wants sorting out.

I am still, at least officially and on paper, a philosopher. How do I *live*? By the seat of my pants and in sometimes roaring confusion. My confusions are feral. They are not a thing to tame without a cost, without some reduction of their nature, so brute yet finely fierce that nature be. This is why I find no consolation in most philosophies that seek to offer some. I can't help but think that they mistake the wild for the tame, or seek to tame the wild where they ought not. As if death is yet another animal to bring to heel with reason, they seek to put a collar on the neck of loss, to contain raw sorrow with a leash, to make a pet of grief. They treat as problem something that I come to think is not. If I were really going to write a book on grief – one that really talked of *grief* and not about the concept – I would need to set the dog of loss off leash, try to make philosophy not fix but live alongside what is feral. If you want some wisdom, don't believe that stuff about ponderous, bearded men in togas deep in concentrated reflection. Sometimes it can just as easily be a wild dog that follows you around.[1]

[1] Apologies to Hemingway and his bicycle policemen.

6

Circle Be Unbroken

I grew up assuming my family was normal, that what we did was just the stuff that people in general do. But now I am old enough and traveled enough to realize that some of what I once considered "ordinary human behavior" belongs instead to family idiosyncrasy. It turns out that my kin did not always initiate me into standard human behavior but something else. Some of what we do is just our own devising, the result of how our collective idiosyncrasies, eccentricities, and even brute preferences worked out. This explains why we sometimes relax on Christmas by target shooting cheap holiday ornaments with my father's old .22. It just happens that we find this more fun than whatever else people can do on an idle afternoon when the more orthodox festivities are finished. But other bits of our behavior have been harder to sort out. They are unusual but seem more fundamental than what idiosyncratic preferences could explain. How we handle our sick, injured, and dead is like this.

For much of my life, I believed that, among human beings generally, it is customary to follow your sick into hospital. When any of my family are hospitalized, it's a given that a crowd will assemble – in the waiting room, the consultation room, the examination room – always as near our patient as we can get. We cluster thickly in moments of genuine medical crisis or high tension. If one of our number is taken to the emergency room or undergoing surgery, we gather en masse. Once the dust of an immediate crisis settles, we tend to thin out, taking unorganized turns setting round the clock. Our ill and ailing are rarely alone, as if when sickness strikes, it takes a vigil to get through it. We do not, however, behave as people keeping vigil.

We're not noticeably purposive about keeping watch or standing by. Neither are we prone to treat medical occasions as inherently momentous or fateful, at least not in any obvious way. Sitting in hospital, we don't turn to prayer or wait in quiet solemnity. We just talk, and talk most about whatever experience has lately thrown into our paths or what memory has mysteriously summoned up for reflection.

During my father's most recent surgery, I wiled away the time discussing with my first cousin once removed whether the buckbrush bedeviling our farm's forested areas has biblical justification. He thought it did, but whether his remedy of choice – a toxic broadcasting of Monsanto chemicals – enjoys biblical warrant we left unaddressed. On one of my grandfather's visits to the emergency room for the stroke-like spells he suffered late in life, my uncles ruefully recalled the summer one of them accidently cut the legs off the other's beagle with the hay mower. My uncle had then owned two beagles, Pete and Repeat, but as much as this incident still sorrowed them both, neither could remember which beagle died, legless, that long ago day. (I think of that dog – Pete, or maybe Repeat – every time I see vultures gathered over a newly made bale, a sure sign the mower caught something that bleeds.)

Conversations such as these also mark what we do where the dead are concerned. When my grandmother died at home in her last illness, my grandfather kept her there for a time so that those of us hastening homeward could arrive and "set with her a bit before the undertakers get her." As I set by my grandmother's corpse in her dim bedroom, my family's distant voices drifted over us from another room. They were talking about a preacher who once stayed at the farmhouse and exercised Grandma's considerable ire because at every meal he was especially greedy in drinking her sweet tea. She handled this masterfully, as was her way, by laying his place with ever-smaller cups, knowing that even his rapacious thirst would draw a line against requesting too many refills. This story ended, as most of ours will do, in laughter, though it was more than a little dimmed, like a ritual recitation of hope no one could just then quite believe in.

We carry conversations such as these straight onward to the grave. Our funeral lunches are filled with them, and we gather annually to have them near our dead. On Decoration Day, we picnic at the small cemetery that abuts our farm, a lonely little patch of rocky acreage no good for farming. Like most in the rural Ozarks, our tiny graveyard bears no signs of the increasingly corporatized funerary industry. The grass gets mowed because my uncle and aunt mow it, and the graves are decorated in whatever fashion we who are left see fit. In truth, we don't even know who all is in there or where. A few decades past, a neighbor with kin buried there got a little too industrious about cleaning it up. He aimed to remove all the rock that can foul a mower blade, but in the process took away many of the broken stones that were all that remained of some of the markers. So, too, family history has always understood there to be Civil War dead in there somewhere, never marked.

We take our annual picnic round an aged oak, tables and lawn chairs haphazardly arranged to make the most of its shade. In the cemetery's sunny regions, a cousin will start a game of baseball. Someone always brings ice cream that will slowly melt while we idly talk of hay, whether it has rained enough to make much or how early in the season my cousin's wretched baler will break down this year. The graves themselves, freshly tidied for the day and new with spring plantings, stand silently a bit apart. While we rarely talk of those laid in them, still we come, all at once, to set with them a bit again, our talk of nothing special, just as it was when they still lived. No one talks of why we do this, nor lately do we even plan it. Where once someone would organize us, calling round to fix a time, of late we just show up near noon, bearing chairs, food enough to share, and inevitably forgetting to bring bags to use when it comes time to carry off our trash.

It naturally did not take long into my adulthood to find that our family practices are so far from commonly shared that they could even be counted peculiar. Many do leave their kin in hospital, unattended for hours at a time by naught but doctors and nurses and other people paid to help. Few at all die at home nowadays, but when they do, the living rarely keep them there for long on purpose. Indeed, I've more than once had the impression that some consider graveyard picnicking macabre. Yet even as I long ago recognized that ours is not standard, regulation-issue human behavior, neither could I escape a deep, inchoate conviction that there was something right and fitting in our ways. Our habits might not be what people do, but still they are what we must do. Sometimes years go by without our shooting ornaments at Christmas, and it simply will not matter, but should anyone be hospitalized alone or the graveyard be empty of the living that last Monday in May, it would seem the world itself was set awry and wrong. I've never known just why this is but think I've lately found an explanation.

I recently came upon a book called *Gone to the Grave* by a reporter named Abby Burnett. In it, she details the death and burial customs common to the Ozarks during the century spanning 1850 to 1950. As I made my way through Burnett's descriptions of now archaic Ozarks practices – setting up with the sick, as well as with the dead, hearty Decoration Day celebrations in graveyards – I found us there.

People in our region did indeed maintain vigils for their sick, for reasons both practical and superstitious. Setting up with the sick meant there would be someone on hand to know when medicine was needed or to administer it, to recognize distress or need, to give or fetch help, and, at the very worst, to see and summon all if the end was coming on. Burnett quotes a nineteenth-century practitioner of the art as saying, "Sometimes there would be a large crowd all night in the sick room. This, however, was not objectionable. The number of people coming in to set up registered the patient's popularity." That seems exactly right to me. Part of the wrongness I've always discerned in the sick abiding alone consists in just the worry that others might think that here is a person about whom no one cares. Worst of all would be for one of ours to pass with neither "loving hands nor pitying hearts" standing near.

More striking still are Burnett's descriptions of Decoration Day. A notice from an 1898 newspaper she cites largely captures the spirit of our own event: "All persons are requested to come and bring a basket well filled with grub, so we can have a good time." And, furthermore: "All persons who come are expected to leave their prejudices and dogs at home." Farm dogs, it seems, have always been the same. Like these long ago sorts, we also hope to picnic without them, but they arrive despite our wishes, for they know that some tender-hearted sort will pass them a bit of chicken. By Burnett's account, these earlier Ozark folks were more deliberate on Decoration Day, dressing up where we come as we are, and featuring some preaching where we just eat and talk. But as it was for them, so it is for us, and "for one day each year at least the cemetery" can still be "a vibrant, colorful place," as well as "of comfort to the community."

To be sure, some of what Burnett describes decidedly does not apply to us, at least not as we presently are, though I now suspect it did apply to our ancestors. In setting with our dead, for example, we are not watching out for cats – apparently, one long ago reason to keep watch over the dead was to fend off the "unspeakable calamity" of feral cats with an appetite for dead flesh. Nor do we build our own coffins or dress our own dead, but the hymns one Opal Arnold Taylor described – "the hauntingly sweet and sad refrains from the old worn song books" – are ours even still. We still look for a touch of comfort in the sweet by-and-by when we must bury our own. Most fundamentally, like one of Burnett's sources says, I think we find it a pleasure "to go to ol' graves 'cause you know your family gathered around that grave at one time, and you know you're walkin' in their tracks there." A lot of what we do, it seems, but walks in tracks laid long ago by kin and neighbors, those who followed these old ways before they were old. At least, that is part of what I can conclude after reading Burnett's study, though there is something still unsettling in all of this, I find.

It is a wonder to find a book like Burnett's. Indeed, it had on me the force of revelation: However much we may depart from the ways now common, I thought, we're not strange; we're *anthropological.* This seems, in several ways and at least on first inspection, a kind of honor, or at least a warrant to be weird. We have stopped trying to cure each other with madstones, calcium deposits filched from the innards of dead deer that our kind once believed to heal the sick, but we carry on with what might count as the better of our traditions. No longer prone to sew ourselves into long johns that we will wear all winter without a wash, our remaining habits are our best, for who could want a world where none who love you are by when you must reach that last necessity? We stand by our ill and ailing, ready for whatever may be needed, and we stand by our dead, even when life has gone on long without them. This has a logic I can like, a suggestion that we are a people grown or growing wise even as we stay within the traces of our past. Yet still I fear the logic does not hold. For it assigns us more purpose than the evidence will bear.

Burnett's book ends with noting, "By the end of World War II almost all Ozark burial customs had been abandoned." As people shifted into styles of work that left little room for the labors of these practices, the practices faded and, so too, the "reasons for the oldest traditions and superstitions had long been forgotten." In this final observation, I saw us again. Even as we persevere, we have stopped doing the most arduous parts of what was once our norm. In my own lifetime, that once-unthinkable bought paper bucket of fried chicken has found its way to our picnic table, and only part of what we eat is cooked by hand. Worse still, Burnett has also got us right in this: We somewhere lost our own logic. I do as my ancestors did, but it took a book to tell me so.

What exactly does it mean to practice the old ways when they are just the only ways you know? In truth, I know less of what to make of us than I did before. Burnett's account of Ozark folkways explains a lot, but while the people she describes did much as we now do, they knew why they did it. Theirs were rituals robust with purpose and with meaning, codified by shared faith and fear. Their vigils sought to fend off death and, where that failed, they could at least fend off the cats. Our version of these is shambolic and confused, like a primitive compulsion we answer as we can – not mutely, to be sure, for there will always be dead dogs and greedy preachers to occupy the spaces that more purposive talk once filled. But we are as a people who answer metaphysical necessity obliquely, doing what we have inherited to do but indirectly and unsure of why we do it. Maybe – the thought alarms me – we are not so anthropological after all.

My dog has the habit most dogs have. When he prepares to settle for a nap, he circles round the spot, his paws making a tight, repetitive circumnavigation over just the place he's picked for sleep. I once heard it said that this ritual trampling of his bed or of a carpet confesses its origin in that time when dogs were wild. A dog circles round where it will lay to first lay down the tall grass, tamping down the strands to make itself a nest. For my dog, of course, the need for this has passed – the bed or carpet is ready there if he wishes to just lay down at once. Yet some primeval internal workings continue on in him, and so he goes on circling.

What if, I wonder, we're like my dog – doing some once meaningful thing because dumb instinct now demands it even as the need for it has passed? Our drifting, idle talk by sickbed, deathbed, and grave is but a sign of tall grass long laid flat, our gathering together an instinctive trampling done on some ultimately brute internal command. That can't be right. Or it can't be all there is, I think. I want for us a purpose and think there is one older even than our ways, one in which I might find sense even when our talk has none.

I come to think the indirection of our talk in crisis, in sorrow and remembrance, is in fact misleading. Better put, it is meaningful misdirection, a way to pose in some serenity. Sometimes the most effective forms of vigilance look like slack – a dog tamping down the tall grass will lay flat a place for rest, but its circling also comprehends all within the circuit. All those wild dogs laying down their grass were also scanning their horizons, looking out for predators that might disturb their rest or worse. Looking ready for rest, in a kind of idle undirected, might be the best pose to take if one is on the watch for danger. I expect it is the same with us.

What sounds like idle talk includes a watchfulness, an eye kept on the horizons in tense expectation of the predator that does and ever will abide. I think I have sighted it sometimes, lurking at the margins, heard its low growl beneath our idle talk. I heard it plainly lately when we gathered in our cemetery, not to picnic but to bury. My uncle then stood where generations of our kind have stood and made the oration that would see off one of us. His scripture on the occasion rehearsed the familiar refrain that death is the last enemy. Yet this is not what he said. He said instead that death is *the* enemy. And there it was and there we were, arrayed against it and once more defeated.

Death has never yielded yet; still and ever it comes for our own. We wait and watch just in case this time we can hold it off as still it takes us, each by each. Someday the graveyard really could be empty on Decoration Day. But it has not yet come for *us*, and this, I think, is the most we can hope.

7

The Invention of Death

The dead leave behind a world transformed because they are not in it, but they also leave behind the world as they designed it. I realized this the first time I was alone in my grandparents' house after their deaths. They were gone, but the clock that marked their hours persisted.

Theirs was a grandfather clock in the old style, full of chains and weights, forceful in announcing itself. Grandpa bought the clock secondhand as a gift for Grandma and it was a noisy extravagance. It is a clock you cannot be near on the hour, at least if you want conversation uninterrupted. As a child, I remarked the clock most on Christmas mornings as it tolled the hours we waited for my grandfather to finish the morning milking and thus the real commencement of Christmas. The milking could not wait, so I would, counting the chimes with restless impatience.

To hear that clock chiming in a house emptied by death was not just loud, but shattering. I thought at once of Christmas and milking and the scent of turkey roasting, all gone. So too, I thought: How could I not have known? How did I fail to anticipate on those Christmas mornings that we would not always go on just so, that the chimes I heard as hastening toward the finish of milking would someday stubbornly chime on, insensate to the end of all milking.

Philip Roth uses the phrase "the invention of death" to describe how death registers when it begins to come for one's own. We live of course with the tedious and unexceptional fact that all people die, but death can be radically novel, some miserably new event loosed upon the world, when it steals those whom one has, unaccountably, assumed would just go on. We mostly just take the world as we are given it and expect it to persist. But it does not persist, and loss is not simple subtraction but some far more complex calculus that transforms the known world itself. These thoughts are obscure, efforts to reach for understanding in experiences visceral and raw.

The basic form of the trouble is just the way that a clock, once my companion in joyfully awaiting Christmas, is transformed by death into a mournful instrument sounding a dirge into a hollow, empty house. And, since death was always there and was not just now invented, one wonders if the dirge was also always there, a sostenuto under all the rest. It was in the first chime after Grandma opened the enormous clock my grandfather had laboriously wrapped in gift paper. It was there as cow after cow was milked, less for the milk itself than to get finished and start Christmas. These are my mournful thoughts.

Death is not just invented upon loss; it invents. Because of how it transfers ownership of worlds, death renders the ordinary strange and changes it into challenge. Death transforms a familiar old clock into a choice: Do we keep it? Do we keep it *going*? The material world another made is abruptly made one's own – to maintain, to undo, to reorganize, to break into parts and distribute. The dead leave us with their things to sort and order, even as death reorganizes what their things might mean. Some of what the dead leave will seem changed by sentiment into charmed objects, symbolic totems of affection without its proper object. Some things will seem burdens to bear, impossible to discard but impossible also to keep.

Some things will just be enigmatic, objects that one did not know existed until the intrusion of death compels the living to intrude into the closets, drawers, and boxes of the dead. Most basically, how do we understand the stuff of lives that have no more use for stuff?

Lately, I have noticed popular articles on "Swedish death cleaning," a practice in which the not-yet-dead do much of the labor their deaths would otherwise create. Anticipating one's approaching end, one casts a critical eye upon one's material world and seeks to thin it, to disperse one's stuff ahead of dying: You reorganize the world so someone else won't have to. The logic of this, and the struggles of the bereaved it seeks to avoid, is captured in an article with a title announcing the hard truth: "Sorry, Nobody Wants Your Parents' Stuff."

To be sure, it is a regrettable truth that many now have far too much stuff. Worse still, much of our abundant stuff is not particularly special but rather mass-produced and cheaply made – things acquired not with care or deep delight but because they were on sale at Target. Death surely does transform such items, too, but they are more likely to be cynically seen: What, after all, was the point of seeking, buying, and keeping *this* when we are mortal? If our homes are filled with impersonal and disposable detritus, then I suppose Swedish death cleaning is an idea as good as any other. But I count myself relieved that my grandparents did no "death cleaning" and instead just died, leaving their world for others to undo. My grief needed the work and whatever understanding work might bring.

Philosophers have always tried to help with understanding, have long carried on about just what death *is*. Indeed, philosophy offers its own variation on "death cleaning," conceptually excising the mental detritus that might inspire irrational fear in we mortals. The most prevalent forms of philosophical death cleaning instruct us that death is nothing. Death will, literally, be the end of me, and so what remains are the questions that attach to such a conclusion: What kind of nothing is it – the kind of nothing that ought to bother me while I still live, or the kind of nothing that ought not? If most of the philosophy books about death published lately are witness, there is a lot to say here. I find none of it to purpose.

One reason death can seem freshly invented in loss is because the death we find in our philosophies is not the one we find in life. The death cleaning our philosophies have yet to do concerns loss – those deaths we must in fact endure and live through. This death is emphatically not nothing, but a novel, awful something – worse still, something we are obliged to *do.* Bereavement inaugurates problems one cannot navigate with thought alone, for the "detritus" is not mental, or not merely so. There is instead a material world at hand and one must find a way to travel it.

Taking apart the world another built illuminates the disquieting frailty of all we build and do. This is useful to see, but it is also a lesson readily found in less laborious ways – the world entire stands ready to deliver the message of transience if we but pay attention. The understanding that interests me is more particular than this. It resides in the strange new intimacy of death's fresh invented world, the way we understand more of what we have lost, even as it's lost, because of what it leaves behind.

When I cleaned out the trunk in my grandparents' bedroom, I found the usual stuff of trunks, old quilts and blankets, but among them there was more. There was an embroidered handkerchief, with "To My Wife, with love from Lynn" worked in tidy chain stitch, its border sewn to note the work was done near Hope, Arkansas, on military maneuvers in 1941. Before my grandfather's hands grew gnarled from milking, he stitched a neat hand. In the hours his army buddies used in playing cards, he worked affection for his new wife Ruby in tan thread. He was never one for cards, but he was always one for Ruby – he told me late in life that once he met her, "it was all over for me." The handkerchief betokened the beginning of his end, the start of "over." I wish I'd seen them then.

The trunk contained his army uniforms too, both rough and dress, each folded carefully and untouched for years. However carefully he'd packed them, though, in his dress uniform pocket he'd left behind an antiquated packet of Juicy Fruit gum. My grandfather must have bought his Juicy Fruit as a young man on some occasion that called for his dress uniform. Perhaps he bought it to freshen his breath. The military did much for his breath. When he joined, his allotted equipment included a toothbrush, the first he ever owned. So too, the army did much for his finances so he could spare the change to buy some gum. All this I could suss out, but what I could not sort was why he didn't finish it. He had a lifelong thrift born of poverty. He was never one to buy what he would not use, never one to buy what he would then forget. That gum wanted a story to go with it, or at least I wanted a story to go with it, some explanation for why it was bought and then why it was never finished.

The handkerchief made sense, the gum did not, except as the modest marker of all I now will never know. I've never much liked Juicy Fruit, but still I wished to try it. Grief is like that – sometimes provoking temptations ridiculous and strange just to have something, anything really, to dilute the intensities of loss. Or perhaps it is that since the world itself has gone strange, one just wants to be strange in it – conceiving a desire to chew gum older than one's mother because it's just not clear what else one can want in the new conditions. I ultimately did not try that gum, though I lingered over the wanting long and hard. In the fancies of sorrow, I decided it was portent and concluded that I ought not chew a portent.

Grief's temptations are many, but in that gum I found the one I like the least: the way the living can consider the dead in some completeness. In their deaths, my grandparents' lives achieved a finished totality, like stories that had run their course and thus like stories I could tell. Their lives began, persisted for a bit, then ended, and I can make of this a sense and order. We the living can be the biographers of our dead, organizing in memory just who they were and who they were to us. This too is an invention of death. The lives of sense and order we can give our dead can only be given them when dead, when they no longer live to swerve away from what our narratives can well permit. When my grandparents lived, I did not understand them, for any sense and order I assigned them was ever subject to revision. There were always bits of them I did not know but they could tell me – bits that, once told, rearranged my sense of who they were. And there were always bits I'd never know, though I could know such bits were there. These were another *sostenuto*, but one I always heard – one can know another well enough to know that there is much one does not know. When they lived, their lives were never what I made of them, but what they did.

The dead leave their things and leave their lives. Death, in its invention, transfers ownership of each. My grandparents' things were mine to sort, their lives now stories I could tell. But because I had the former, I could set aside the latter and tarry longer in what was not yet lost, the tones of all I cannot know humming through their things. I could hesitate and linger with what was neither mine nor memory's but instead the stuff of mystery. This, then, is understanding, if there is any to be had.

Something I have lately done may trace out well beyond its rightful temporal place. Perhaps I have left something in a pocket, or in a drawer or trunk forgotten. Perhaps it waits there now, to be discovered when I am dead, a grandchild I cannot yet imagine the one to find and puzzle over it. She'll want a story too, and she won't have anyone left to tell it either. We live in mystery, and even when the dead are gone, this bit of them abides. Death does not invent this, but neither does it end it.

8

Fine for Caius

When I was once teaching a class about death, about Epicurus' storied argument that "death is nothing to us," I paused to let a student speak. He'd raised his hand in urgency and I expected the sort of thing one does: He'd have an objection to old Epicurus or a question needing answer. But instead my student cried out in a kind of agony: *We're all going to die!* Yes? I asked, in startled puzzlement. *No, but really. I mean, we are ALL going to DIE!* He wailed it out again and more emphatically because, put plainly, we are and he abruptly understood this, understood it radically, existentially and viscerally. I then had the splitting-off experience common in my teaching career. I externally carried on being the philosopher and intellectual, while internally I balked. He's right, I thought, we are going to die, and what the hell are we doing *here*?

In the 1950s, the sociologist Geoffrey Gorer published an article called "The Pornography of Death," in which he lamented the popularity of the horror comic and, more broadly, entertainments featuring violent death. He claimed that violent entertainments indicate a "prudery" about death. Like sexual pornography, he argued, fantastical simulations of violent death function as "substitute gratification." Both obscure the emotions and meaning we might assign to events in favor of what are merely bodily theatrics, unrealistic "fantasy" of ever escalating raw sensation. He theorizes that the appeal of pornographies, whether of sex or death, arises where we have made the human experiences they purport to depict taboo. He says that "people have to come to terms with the basic facts of birth, copulation, and death, and somehow accept their implications; if social prudery prevents this being done in an open, dignified fashion, then it will be done surreptitiously" – that is, through "pornography." Gorer himself, to be clear, is not a prude but, rather, recognizes that the death one encounters in violent entertainments is not the death that one encounters in life. It is all and only sensation and sensationalized. Death is frightening, but *DEATH!!!* affords a thrill and, if you see enough of it, can even become quite boring. Being thrilled or bored by death are both a kind of power. One need only to consider the experiential difference between watching a rip-roaring shoot-'em-up film and one depicting a single slow death from cancer to catch at Gorer's point. *DEATH!!!* is fun; death is not. And enjoying watching *DEATH!!!* can mislead you about death, make you think it less daunting than it is.

Whatever one might make of Gorer's argument, I prize its recognition that one of the headiest struggles in thinking about death is just trying to discern whether one is really thinking about *death* rather than a convenient counterfeit, some largely fictional substitute that is more easily managed than the thing itself. When I read philosophy about death and when I myself have tried to write some, I often worry that whatever it is we philosophers are carrying on about, it isn't really death. To be sure, we don't go in for the sensational and fantastical. Instead, we favor high abstraction: not death made bloody, but death made bloodless. But like the horror comic that troubles Gorer, our style of death too often seems detached from all that might or could really come to pose a threat. The philosopher's death will never titillate and thrill, but it certainly can bore. Turned into a concept, it hardly seems a thing to fear. Perhaps this is but a hazard of the craft itself. If one's allegiance is to reason, you want a foe that reason can defeat, and death turned into concept seems like that.

I consider that philosopher who so horrified my student, Epicurus, a kind of standard-bearer for the ways that clean abstraction can make good arguments that, for all of that, somehow miss their mark. His argument that "death is nothing to us" is well reasoned and, because of this, has long occupied philosophers who think on death. Death can be "nothing" because it just *is* an end – of consciousness, of existence, of the person who, only while she lives, can find things bad. Epicurus reasoned that since death will end me, I should not fear it: It simply isn't rational to fear what one will not experience. The trouble I have with Epicurus is not the soundness of his reasoning but instead all that it leaves out.

Death might be just a terminus, but it's one we travel toward, and I expect that how you get there matters. All the stuff that precedes death, the dying, can go well or ill, and it may be hard to tell what "well" can mean here. More emphatically, like most philosophy that grew out of Greece, Epicurus underestimates how death features in a life, understanding it as but my end. I will die – of course I will – but before that comes, I will first suffer the deaths of others. The reasoning that could help me meet my own end is of little use when others do. When others die, it is not nothing. The deaths of others are just those deaths we must and do experience, deaths one must survive and, somehow, endure. They are a terrible, living *something*. Where life is long enough, they are multiple somethings. The problem here, I think, is not really death. The problem is *deaths*, the serial losses a life accumulates, each so achingly particular and each the start of some new loneliness. I can't quite convince myself that Epicurus ever felt this.

While generations of philosophers have since spilt lots of ink writing of death in ways that Epicurus would have liked, some others seem to have a trouble more like mine, a struggle to make the concept answer to the facts and to experience. Lucretius writes as one who heartily accepts what Epicurus offers, but he writes it up in poetry rather than cool reason because, he says, bitter medicine goes down better with some honey brushed round the lip of the glass. Despite his professed affinity with Epicurus, though, I think he ends up doing something else. Where Epicurus can be dry as dust, Lucretius' work is colored all through with vivid natural imagery that readily awakens both glorious awe and dreadful terror. His is a world of both lambs at play and people dying of the plague, and it's the latter that seem to carry the day. His poem ends with graphic, aching scenes of awful human suffering – not just people dying miserably, but frantic mourners fighting over wood they need to burn their dead – and these are then just left there on the page. *Death* is not defeated, even if the *concept* gets a trouncing. Death abstracted might be nothing, but death in fact is not. At the end of Lucretius' poem, there is no salving comfort given, no sense that with a little more intellectual work this could all come right. The end of that poem even led some to think Lucretius had gone mad. Tennyson famously thought so. He wrote a poem that has Lucretius reaching for a kind of rational peace, but instead of this Lucretius finds that an "unseen monster lays his vast and filthy hands upon my will, wrenching it backwards into his." Tennyson's Lucretius stretches reason taut as it can go, but finds the answering snap back to experience more than he can bear. Death turns out not to be a concept and, in the words of another Roman, Seneca, treating it as such can leave you "facing a lion's charge armed with an awl." My student crying out in horror at our common doom could find no protection in the awl I was then handing him.

In Tolstoy's *The Death of Ivan Ilyich*, Ivan suffers the slow revelation that his end is coming on and all that he had before understood comes to seem like misplaced complacency – it is all falsehood and false confidence. He recalls the well-worn syllogism he learned as a child: "All men are mortal. Caius is a man. Therefore, Caius is mortal." This is but the tightest logic, undeniable and right. But it is also useless for Ilyich, for while Caius is a man, he is also and at once, just *any* man, a placeholder instead of a person. And none of us has yet lived as such a one, a fact that arrives for Ilyich in all its horror. Caius can be mortal, but only because he could be anyone and thus is really no one at all:

> For the man Caius, man in general, it was perfectly correct; but he was not Caius and not man in general . . . Was it for Caius, the smell of the striped leather ball that Vanya had loved so much? Was it Caius who had kissed his mother's hand like that, and was it for Caius that the silk folds of his mother's dress had rustled like that? . . . Caius is indeed mortal, and it's right that he die, but for me, Vanya, Ivan Ilyich, with all my feelings and thoughts – for me it's another matter. And it cannot be that I should die. It would be too terrible.

Ilyich is shocked to find that he must die not least because he carries within him all that is particular to him, all that refuses cool rationality and bland remove.

Tolstoy presents Ivan Ilyich as something like a tragic fool, a man quite deeply self-deceived. He has always been mortal, but declines to see this until his death is closing fast upon him. Yet I've never been able to entirely begrudge Ivan his belatedness. He's late to knowledge, but, then, aren't we all? And maybe we can only be so? I don't want to think so, but still I have my doubts. I can know, with reason made impeccable, that those I love will die, but it's hard to make of this a fact that forms experience itself. Reason tells me people die, but it cannot well assay what this is *like*.

I have not yet found for death and loss a language that will suit. Death seems a thing like love, the kind of thing that does not hold up well when stripped of all its particulars. The devilry of both lives in their details. Abstraction renders both generic, but in experience they are radically distinct and acutely specific. We live in detail, and so we have to die that way as well. And because we also love in detail, we lose that way as well. It doesn't matter that people die; it matters too much that little Vanyas do.

9

At the Orthocenter

The book on death and grief that I was meant to write has gone all sideways. I have kept writing, but not the way I meant to do, nor with any result I can in confidence trust. I have instead produced a fun-house mirror image of the thing I had set out to write – the philosopher in me is *there*, just stretched and strange. If I can't make her look the way she ought, maybe I can let her be the way she tends?

These were my desperate, hopeful thoughts when I gave some of the fun-house "chapters" to my husband, hoping they might do something like the work I had originally intended. It would be a quixotic kind of book, but maybe it would work? And maybe Garret could confirm that and save me from my ongoing agonies with the staid and conventional book I was supposed to write. Garret has been my first and best reader for years, able to divine what I was after and remark on it in ways to get me nearer to it. But about the pages that I gave him, our usual ways of good exchange have not worked as they most often do.

I've always mildly envied the Buddha, and not only for the obvious reasons. His enlightenment must surely have been nice, but it's his rhetorical strategy I just now most envy. In interactions with his students, he sometimes refused to answer questions because, he said, some questions are "questions which tend not to edification." After reading what I'd written, Garret asked me some of those. He wanted to know why my "book" has no proper introduction, and if maybe I could add one. He wanted to know whether these short "chapters" could be read in any order – that is, if there were really any through lines binding one to one that would come next. He wanted to know, most vexingly of all, for whom this book is written. "Who are you writing it for?" he asked. "Who would you expect to read it?" I hasten to say that none of these were asked in the tone of criticism. Rather, his was of a wary bemusement, a cautious kind of wondering that, for all its hesitation, still said more than I then wished to hear.

Who would read it? On its own, this question need not be a fright. Anyone who writes may well wish her work at home with any who might like it. But *who would read it?* also cuts another way. It is a question closely adjacent to another, much more vexing: *Who would buy it?* For pages to become a book, someone needs to buy it and, for this, not just anyone will do. One needs a publisher, and therein lies so much that cannot edify. My experiences with publishing would tell me I am doing this all wrong.

Some few years ago, an agent courted me to write a book, but nothing came of it. He was apparently charmed by the tragicomic potential of a philosopher-cum-farmer. I still do not entirely know just what he wanted, but it wasn't what I had, episodic essays that offered nothing close to a clear "point," a thing he thought I needed. I felt he wanted me to be a figure more tidily amusing than I am – say, a philosopher making mistakes most stupid while farming, or a farmer pausing in her labor for deep thoughts. At any rate, none of this was of account because my style itself was just all wrong. Almost no one can hope to publish essays. Only those "selected to be in the circle of cool" or Marilynne Robinson can pull it off.

Whatever the "circle of cool" looks like to publishers in New York, I am not in it, a lesson I had already learned.

Some few years ago, when I published a philosophical book on rudeness aimed at the general reader, my publisher declined to market it outside those rarefied domains peculiar to academic philosophy. When I confessed my disappointment, I was invited to a conference call with someone from their "marketing team," a call I'd like now to forget. The marketer took me as a kind of pupil and exhorted me to "seize the initiative:" I should arrange public readings with my local bookstores and thereby "get the word out." I would be amazed "at what a little word of mouth can do." I was just then sitting in sight of the only bookseller in my area, having driven the fifteen miles from my farm to the nearest town, there to sit in the McDonald's parking lot and access the cell signal that would make the phone call work. As I gazed out my windshield and across the highway bypass at the Walmart, I entertained the prospect of reading there aloud. Perched in the aisle among the Amish romances that sell so well round here, I would be tempted to a preacher's cadences in reading. I'd want to declaim the words and make them loud, my "word of mouth" at volume. That the people in our little country town would be too polite to stop me made it all seem pointless – they did not need my book on rudeness. When I told the marketer of my present limitations where "local booksellers" and public readings were concerned, she exhorted me to join Twitter. I never did that either. Because of this experience, my later talk with the literary agent felt like an unhappy déjà vu.

The book, if there should be one, would have to take a structure and a form that he and then a publisher could sell. The agent spoke in terms of "pitches" and of "hooks," ways to link me to other people's sold words so that mine could better sell by the connection. He spoke, too, of our pinning down just what *need* my book might meet. This style of talk was one I could at least find familiar as it informs the academic writing

I have long done for my job. In scholarship, most needs are framed in metaphors of sight and gaps: What is it that you, dear scholar, have seen that others have not yet spotted but would do well to see? What gap in the literature will your work now bridge? The gaps that my imagined book might close were gaps I might think better open, sights no one now can really need to see. At least, I could not quite get round how to explain just why some faraway and so-far-fictional reader might need to know about my grandmother's first bra or that time a coyote trailed my tractor path across a field. There is all detail and no idea to it. The want of some idea might even be the point and purpose of it all, but a point and purpose then no use at all.

Perhaps because I so badly floundered in my efforts to produce a pitch, the agent tried to help me out. He complimented samples of my writing, but too often in a language that I struggle still to understand. In his judgment, my work sat at the "orthocenter" of three other authors, each unlike the other, but each successful in their way. The encouragement was pleasant, but it came alongside suggestions I could not like. The book the agent described as one he thought me well made to write sat at the orthocenter of conceptual art, caricature, and pathos. I was affronted by it and by the absurdity that it would make of me.

Years ago, a friend of mine remarked in tones of fiery passion his distaste for conceptual art. "What if," he implored, "I were to go to Central Park in New York City, bring a shovel and my work boots. I would then dig a hole. And then, having dug that hole, I would fill it up again." He paused and looked long and meaningfully at me. "See!" he declared. "Don't you see?! Once I have said this and you have entertained it as an idea, I have no need to do it! The mere idea is everything and more than enough!" Conceptual art, he insisted, depended entirely on idea, on whatever oddity-made-statement digging a hole in Central Park to fill it up conveyed. It did not need to be done; indeed, doing it would be superfluous, surplus to requirements and, because of this, more work than it could ever be worth.

It would even likely be disappointing as a thing to do. And so it was also with the book the agent seemed to want from me. State your incongruities plainly, and they obviate the need for further labor. If I tell you I am a philosopher-turned-farmer, there's not much more you need to see.

My engagements with the agent soon diminished and then stopped altogether. In the current idiom, he "ghosted" me. I confessed over email to being at a loss, and there our exchanges found their end. I could see he knew his business, but his business was not, is not, mine. Whatever initial excitement I had felt had passed into frustration, yet the lack of a reply from him still did a nasty kind of work. One cannot like the feeling that another has so given up on one's purported "promise" that he cannot even say so.

Publishing and all that it entails is just a burden I don't well bear. It isn't just the need for tidy pitches and sharp hooks, but the transformation of myself that the process would induce. So much of what the stock advice involves consists in strategies to seek and keep attention, a commodity for which one must be prepared to fight and scramble. Injunctions to join Twitter or other social media are ubiquitous, for this is how one so-far-unnoticed may come to the right attention or at least begin to make the necessary contacts. One should seek to "circulate" among the internet's literary scene, presumably to display wit or wisdom that could catch and hold a wandering online eye. Unwilling still to take this awful step, I turned to the duller advice to read widely in the literary journals and magazines, though read widely I did not. For it was soon clear that I have none of the urbanity that they appear to like. Should I try to write a thing made well to suit, I would need a new personality and history, a new diction too; I would need to be so much less provincial and altogether more modishly sophisticated than I am. I'd have to somehow lose my native tongue, forget I cut my linguistic teeth on a steady diet of southern idiom and the King James Bible.

Lest I appear here to lament the state of publishing, the citified elite that work therein, or even the capitalist imperative to make what sells, I hasten to say that I am myself the bigger problem. I am well acquainted with the ways that subcultures will have their own distinctive tastes, their idiosyncratic patterns and preferences, and an underlying logic that those outside it cannot understand. I am, after all, an academic – one schooled well enough in all the mysteries of a culture at least as peculiar as publishing. I also thereby know that to succeed in such a culture one sometimes must just put oneself in harness and settle in to pull the plow, no matter what one thinks of it or its necessity. One must sometimes but capitulate and accept the way things work. But I do so tire of "the way things work." Having mastered one such way, I am all opposition to another. My initial hope to write in ways that academics usually don't was meant to shrug the harness off, not for another but for freedom. I come to see that among the worst to happen to my writing was that agent. Here was another harness, but of a more pernicious sort.

For long months after I encountered that agent, the persona I assigned to him and all his kind lurked everywhere my words might go. He would tell me "that can't sell" and importune "but what would be the pitch?" I sometimes tried to write as he suggested but was then like fertile soil all paved over, a place where nothing grows. I was forever trying to locate myself at orthocenters but was plagued by all the distasteful things that I can name in sets of three. My mood sat in the vicinity of where self-doubt, gloom, and opposition intersect.

Who would read it? Garret is not wrong to ask, however unedifying my answer. Socrates claimed that wisdom lay in knowing when one did not know. The only way that's left to me, I think, is to pretend that I am wise.

10

Ary a Word

My great-grandmother Dovie might have said there's "ary" words to suit the stuff of grief and loss. She would have said that, but I cannot. For "ary" has been excised from my family's working vocabulary. Dovie's daughter, my grandmother Ruby, made sure enough of that, taking care that she and hers would steer away from hillbilly speech and diction. Ruby was even sometimes visibly pained to hear Dovie speak. Dovie grew up in a place called Dark Holler, and sounded like she had. Her speech was littered all through with words that told on her as one without an education and without means. Ruby reared my mother not to talk that way. Yet my mother remembers. A few years back, she gave me a book of Ozark speech – not a dictionary exactly, but one to feature lists of words and phrases once familiar but now gone, or going, out of use. The book contained my mother's marginalia, where alongside several entries she wrote "Mimi," the name that we of her descendants used for Dovie. My mother never uses "ary," but she remembers it and pencils in the one who used it. It is not, for her, a curiosity in a book, but a word once and no longer for the ear, a grandmother's word, remembered in a grandmother's voice. I think this is part of the problem when it comes to loss and what could be a language for it. Sometimes loss just means losing language.

It is of course true that grief can steal your words – crying, at least as I tend to do it, is sound made where language stops. Grief can be altogether too physical for words. But that is not what I here mean. Instead, I have in mind the way that loss can register in words that death steals along with our own dead. Perhaps because I treasure words and try to choose them deliberately, I begrudge death this. I call it *stealing* because that is how it strikes me. The words are not misplaced, nor forgotten; they got *taken*. And you can no more get them back than you could a wallet stolen. My thoughts here turn to thievery because it was talk of thieves that would not be called so that led me first to feel this.

Not long before he died, I sat in hospital with my grandfather, keeping him company as he awaited, gowned and gaunt, whatever the doctors might do. Before he sent me home to catch a bit of rest, he pointed me to the wardrobe and asked me to take his wallet home. He worried, he said, that "some ornery fella might come in while I sleep and get into my britches and I'd lose my pocketbook." This was then no kind of odd, but just the way my grandpa talked. But of course, when you're on the cusp of losing something, you remark it. The ordinary can't stay so when you start to see it how it really is – not a permanent and unexceptional part of the world, but a fleeting visitation almost over. The world of ornery fellas never was the world itself, even if you took it so. Your own britches can become mere "pants," against your will. By the time I was carrying my grandfather's wallet home from the hospital to save it from any wandering thieves, I had already long seen his mortality. I just hadn't, till that evening, heard all that would go with him, all those ornery and old fellas.

When my grandfather died, so too did some old fella. Near but tamer kin to some ornery fella, some old fella was the protagonist in many of my grandfather's stories, featuring especially in tales about people who mess up. Some old fella built his farmhouse chimney out of rock that exploded when heated, a fact he belatedly discovered on lighting his first fire and burning down his house entire. Some old fella used poison ivy leaves for toilet paper when an urgency outdoors took him by surprise. In short, some old fella was feckless and luckless. All throughout my life, my grandfather told stories of him, sometimes just to note how people can go wrong so we could use them as a caution, but more often just because some old fella was also reliably a man about whom we could well make sport. He was always getting up to foolish things – accidentally shooting his own dog or being run down by an angry sow – to make us feel our own faults somewhat less. Whatever travails we had suffered, at least we'd not burnt down the house or killed the dog. To be sure, my family still whiles away the time, especially that interregnum that follows a fine shared meal, telling stories rich with human folly. But the stories lack their once singular and near-mythical protagonist. They're stories of people with proper names. Some old fella is in the graveyard with my grandpa.

I doubt my grandpa knew that he spoke in ways most distinctive. He just spoke the ways he spoke, freely casting life's intensities in a characteristically gentle, archaic understatement. As his strength and health began to fail, he'd never bemoan his increasing weakness but remark the change in tanks of fuel. Where once he could wield his chainsaw, cutting firewood for stretching hours, in his nineties he had only "one tank in me." Once the saw was empty, so was he. I only once heard him speak of his own oncoming death. Of it, all he said was that he would "prefer to abide a little longer." Since we always had to pray before a meal, I'd hope he'd be the one to do it. A tendency to understatement, I suspect, may be an aid if one will pray. For my grandfather, all of human sin and folly, all our misdeeds and mistakes, would find tidy sum in his asking God to "help us to leave undone the things we shouldn't do."

That does pretty much cover it, and nicely too. Lately, the bit of his praying that most sounds and resounds in my thoughts is what he would pray in church to summon up some blessing on the preacher ahead of his sermon: "Give the preacher a happy recollection of the things that he has studied." Grandpa isn't here to plead for me, but I, too, could use some happy recollection of the things that I have studied. But all I have just now is this, echoing trails of sound long gone, all voice and no idea. The idea of an *idea* is itself a sound to drown out all else that should here follow.

When my grandfather had conceived some mad plan both ingenious and daring, he'd simply say, "I have an idea." This phrase was sign and signal that something truly novel was about to be afoot – that something that never should work was about to be worked upon the world, that marvels soon would follow. But I have to interject here and insist upon precision. My grandpa's pronunciation of "idea" was never proper – it sounded like *i-dee,* with the stress upon the *i.* He did not have ideas, but *i-dees.* My present compulsion to clarify this owes to my lifelong sense that "ideas" and *i-dees* are not the same. The first is something anyone can have; the other is a word to inaugurate something entirely new into the world. One cannot like the end of all *i-dees.*

I have now gone far adrift from what I'd meant to write – something about how language is never only words but sensibility, and it's a sensibility that death will take when it takes the ones who use the words. I wanted to write that when my grandfather died, the *atmospherics* of life suffered an alteration that I did not like, the world became a place that much less infused with wry humility about ourselves and what we do. But really I can't find it much in me to write all that. I have no *i-dee,* just echoes of a once familiar language never mine but in which I had some happy share. I'd rather here record the words themselves, but even that really does not suit. They were not really words meant for pen or pixels, but words for voice.

It bothers me to have all this language lost and gone. It bothers me more to burden pages upon pages with the dulled and dulling artifice that forms my learned, professional voice. That voice is what my book on grief most needs. That voice could lift into generalized (and thus wholly inadequate) abstraction the problem of languages going lost when those who speak them perish. See – the strange voice unhappily mine intones – language is part of constructing the world as we experience it, what sense we make of it and, also, the more nebulous felt quality of what the world seems *like.* Lose the speaker, lose the language. Lose the language, lose the world. That's an idea I could develop into a chapter for my book on grief, an idea I could trace through several philosophers, historical and wise. I could do that, but I won't. I am altogether too haunted by the version of myself that would develop under such a task: I might not blow up my own house with sedimentary rock built in the chimney, but I'd be doing something like. Some old fella put in a book all the ways we suffer with our griefs.

11

Kill All the Chickens

When I was in graduate school, a professor came upon me listening to music in my headphones. The music had stunned me, and it must have shown in my face, for he asked if something was wrong. I told him no, but explained that I'd just heard the "Ode to Joy." I can't recall exactly what I said next, but it involved my enthusing about what a wonderful "song" it was, and asking if he had ever heard it. He had. And his response alerted me to the fact that it was not usual to call it a "song." The professor's manner was kind, but it was impossible not to notice his shock that here was a creature seeking a PhD who had never before heard the "Ode to Joy." This was but one of my earliest signals that I lacked the standard cultural and class equipage of academe.

Early in my career, I regularly mispronounced words, for the vocabulary of academia was one I had only encountered in books – its language was emphatically not the stuff people I knew said out loud. I was once congratulated on my "bravery" for not training out my "rustic accent," never mind I didn't know, until then, that I had one. More recently, I was asked to develop a seminar on class bias. I am a philosopher, and since I do not study class bias, the request surprised me. I later discovered I was chosen for my "unique" life experience, my perceived lower-class origins. Even now, people casually ask me at conferences where I am from, in a way that suggests they are struggling to place the unusual. A student once marveled that I "talk like Faulkner." Another, prompted by a course evaluation to "describe this instructor in one word," recorded: "y'all."

Before entering academia, I wasn't terribly aware of my class. My family had made out pretty well relative to many of our neighbors and even kin. But judgments of "doing pretty well" depend of course on your point of comparison and, at any rate, the cultural capital my upbringing supplied relied on a different currency than what gets spent in academe. In academia, people carry Beethoven in their pockets like so much loose change. My pockets weren't empty, sure, but they were mostly stuffed with commercial jingles. So I often felt broke in a land of the wealthy, a cultural pauper among the aristocracy. To use the coin of the realm, you could say I had "imposter syndrome" – that perception that one is not adapted for one's role, that one does not really belong or pass muster.

I still lack the cultural stuff to fit seamlessly in academic environments. Yet even as I often feel ill-fitted, using the archetype of an "imposter" to explain myself to myself has never offered me much value. "Imposter syndrome" is a conceptual construct rendered in the language and sensibility of the very thing I feel ill-fitted for. It is an academic term, after all, and seems like an affliction for the higher orders, a malady that you have to come up a bit in the world to develop. Most importantly, I can vividly imagine the withering look my grandmother would offer if someone dared to suggest she suffered from "imposter syndrome."

My grandmother Ruby was both a farm wife and a professional woman. The family dairy could not be sustained absent someone taking a job in town, and so Ruby acquired an entry-level position with the Department of Children and Family

Services. By the time she retired, she had ascended the ranks and served as its director for years. In an era that largely denied women such roles, she had become a professional of real stature and consequence. And she assiduously sought to fit the part, reliably turned out for work in immaculate business suits and sensible heels, polished and groomed, and pristinely arranged. To the unaware, Ruby never would have been taken for a farm wife, and that was precisely the point. She wanted to be received as a woman of class and as someone at home *in town*, though this took work and, at least once, not a little violence.

Ruby's car for commuting was stored in the farmhouse garage. Since the garage was most often open, though, the chickens had a habit of shading in there and, not to put too fine a point on it, shitting in there. Finally, after too long enduring the choice between cleaning the car of chicken scat or driving it soiled to work, she emerged from the garage one day and called out calmly to her eldest son: "Bob, kill all the chickens." This he did, and never again did her car betray her efforts to pass as "town."

I sometimes recite this silently to myself when I am in academic environments: "Bob, kill all the chickens." I find it functions as a bit of truly useful self-therapeutics, a mantra for lower class passing among the smarter set. I'll never achieve my grandmother's radical self-command and impeccable grooming, but if tempted by feelings of "imposter syndrome," I aspire to her wickedly cynical gaze.

Ruby did kill all of the chickens or, rather, have them killed. But this should not be seen as a particularly dramatic technique for battling imposter syndrome. For her solution of choice could not possibly be more *farm* – town women, after all, don't generally have the stuff and stomach to command the slaughter of hens as an aside as they make their way to work. Ruby's lack of hesitation or ruminating is at odds with that insecure, inner scrutiny of oneself against an imagined external measure. Imposter syndrome is an existential malady; chicken killing is an existential refusal, a way of holding in reserve that fierce, unfitted part of oneself. In the latter, the "imposter" is subversive, not passively feeling out of sorts in unaccustomed environments but actively pulling who-the-hell-knows-what just out of sight. I imagine Ruby that day she had the chickens slain arriving at work unruffled and polished, but with some heady dissident mischief in her eye.

"Imposter syndrome" describes a problem I don't especially wish to solve. Its remedy is to recognize that one does in fact *belong*. Yet I can't convince myself I want to fully belong – indeed, I would experience belonging as a loss. The reasons for this are several, though all converge on a conviction that being ill adapted has a value I would not forfeit.

Academia has long been reserved for the upper class – for those with financial and, especially, cultural capital – and this limits what academics typically see or, more accurately, admit to seeing. Even though many of us do not belong to the normalized, cultured class of the stereotype, our modes of interaction often encourage us to talk as if we do. Put plainly, if you do have chickens, best get the scat off your car. The result is that the world we assay looks cleaner, simpler and more pristine than it really is. Some of my own dissatisfaction with belonging results from a restless critical impulse, a desire to see what cleanliness is obscuring.

In my field, philosophy, we have few historical sources that engage the rural and agrarian, far less the poor. This deficiency means that the points of reference we do possess earn an outsized authority, even if they show us little. Call this the *Walden* phenomenon.

When other philosophers learn I have a farm, they often invoke Thoreau's *Walden*. This text seems the philosopher's Rosetta stone for country life. I am in great sympathy with cultured sorts who long for the agrarian – indeed, in many respects, I am one now. Yet I can only tolerate *Walden* if I read it fancifully, as deliberate self-satire. Or if I construct a running sub-commentary of what Thoreau's truly country neighbors must have thought. There may be some who farm who enjoy Thoreau, but I am not one.

When Thoreau engages in self-congratulation – "How many mornings, summer and winter, before yet any neighbor was stirring about his business, have I been about mine!" – I marvel at the unreflective ease with which he equates simply tramping about with the work of his laboring neighbors. "No doubt," he continues, "many of my townsmen have met me returning from this enterprise, farmers starting for Boston in the twilight, or woodchoppers going to their work." No doubt. Perhaps those farmers and woodchoppers have lain abed late because their prior day's labor required longer rest. More likely, they've been up and about doing chores Thoreau lacks the experience to imagine.

Thoreau's country life is mannered, but worse still are canonical sources that romanticize not simply rural life, but poor, countrified people. Whether it is Rousseau's rustic or Tolstoy's Russian peasant, the country folk one encounters most often in literature tend to be admirable only insofar as they are rather simple-minded, unburdened by self-awareness. Tolstoy's Gerasim in *The Death of Ivan Ilyich* is a paradigm case.

As servant to the existentially tortured and dying Ilyich, Gerasim is reconciled to mortality. His consciousness is uncluttered, guileless, and unambitious in what it seeks to query, much less understand. He takes what comes as it comes. This makes him compassionate in a tale of middle-class false consciousness and woe – but no one could want to *be* him. Humming beneath any admiration inspired by Gerasim's stoical simplicity is John Stuart Mill's dictum: Better to be Socrates dissatisfied than a pig satisfied.

Recently, the romanticized peasant-simple has yielded to another, darker idea. The pigs, it turned out, were not that satisfied, and now they have dragged us all down in the political mire. The image is no longer unsullied simplicity but befouled by bigotry, misogyny, and cruelty. This too is a stereotype, and one that, however different, achieves force precisely in its distance – and this, too, works to keep the ivory tower pristine, for even fewer now are likely to confess low origins.

Academia's representations of the poor and rural inspire an oppositional impulse in me – a resistance to seeing *people like mine* as *people like that*, as people tidily captured, whether quaint or corrupt, pitiable or pitiless. Assimilation in academia entails the denial of one's own experience and history. It demands sacrifice, a willingness to shed complexity and, along with it, possibilities. It's the possibilities I begrudge the most. At least some of what we shed we really ought to keep.

When I took over the farm following my grandfather's death, I initially despaired at all the loose bits and pieces that littered the place. Wire was my special enemy, for the barns were everywhere cluttered with it – wire salvaged from telephones, from appliances, from who-could-tell-where. I accumulated buckets of wire with a plan to dispose of it. Mercifully, I never got round to it, for I quickly learned the uncommon worth of wire. For example, it presently holds the muffler to my truck, secures the busted PTO cover on my brushhog and seams caging around fruit tree saplings, the better to protect them from the depredations of deer. My only concern about wire now is that I might need more.

The stock images sometimes used to depict the pitiable conditions or pathologies of the rural poor – images of home-places surrounded by wreckage and "trash" – tell a bigger story if you know how to read them. The broken-down car in the yard contains parts that still have use in them if need arises. That rusty freezer on the porch probably contains the dog's food, since nothing beats an old freezer for storing feed where unsanctioned animals can't get at it. Put plainly, if there is wire everywhere, there's probably a reason. And if you can't see the reason, there's probably a reason for that too.

Farming's impulse to make do, and to make more of what you have, encourages in me vitalizing mental habits that are at odds with the orderly practices of academe. In life, it is a general good to see the strange, non-standard potentials in things, to use something built for one purpose for an entirely different purpose. So, too, it's a plain good to fix what's broke, whether mechanical or intellectual. And it's good to become accustomed to a world that won't always yield, to the recalcitrant material stuff that cares not for our larger, or even smaller, purposes – wire can't, after all, do *everything*, no matter how much of it you have.

These are all, to be sure, advantages of a non-specific sort, and I struggle to say more exactly what my life background and farmwork have added to my academic endeavors. I have yet to find use for commercial jingles, but I have sought most avidly those bits of intellectual wire that can tie together complexities I carried in with me and have declined to abandon.

The philosophies that make most sense to me are not the common run in academic philosophy, those canonical sources so often touted as essential. Formally, I am expert in early Confucian ethics, with a tidy list of publications that focus most especially on Confucian approaches to grief and to the deep dependencies of human beings, the ways we become what we are by way of our relations to others.

Informally, I study that which can render into sense the immense piles of rock on my farm. Those rocks did not form piles on their own but represent generations of effort to wrench usable farmland from inhospitable hills. Every rock in those mounds was carried there by people – my people. My academic philosophy is an effort to do justice to those rocks, to catch at the modest monuments of human dependency on which shared well-being rests. I work to catch at how nothing made is made in solitude, to catch at all the sorrows of surveying those rocks when the carriers of rock are dead. And to catch, at last, the exquisitely prosaic longing to add to the piles for the ones who come next. Like my ancestors, I'll spend my farming life moving rock. Philosophy, I suppose, has helped me say why, and why I wouldn't have it otherwise.

Fundamentally, I resist scavenging through my philosophy to identify the bits fostered in farmwork. For I find naught but irritation in trying. Too many philosophers already profess to locate value in experiences – exercise, leisure reading, yoga, or travel – precisely because they aid in advancing the intellectual enterprise. This inevitably subordinates the thing praised; experiences become valuable only to the extent they are *good for* the real work or, as I mentally style it, The Work. I balk at the need to show how the hard problem of fixing my alternator will improve my chances of solving the hard problem of consciousness, or to show how a bit of farm labor can unlock philosophical secrets. In truth, I harbor strong doubts about which of these really ought to be counted as The Work. This doubt is one of my most treasured non-standard supplies, the chicken I will never kill.

Academic philosophy likes to talk about itself in resonant tones of high ambition and noble aspiration, as though philosophy is that which indubitably matters most. I have no complaint with those who place their philosophical work at the center of their lives, but our professional atmosphere is sometimes choked with talk that assumes this disposition is the right and only way. To normalize and conform is to become fluent in re-casting one's projects and activities in servitude to The Work. At its worst, it pitches toward scorn of other lives and slips into a tendency to condescend, as if philosophy is the light and all else is darkness.

Sometimes, as in my grandmother's life, the raw exigencies of existence send one to town for work and, it turns out, one is good at the work one finds. This pattern, reproduced in academic environments, can tempt a success narrative, a variation on the Horatio Alger myth. The simple or sullied abandons the darkness for light and, in entrepreneurial fashion, accumulates the stores of cultural capital to which others are merely born. At her best, she completely passes, becoming indistinguishable from the native Brahmins. Even failures to pass may contribute to the myth. Having a non-standard beginning in academia can raise the anxious specter of the imposter, but it can also ground special praise. One has, after all and against the odds, come far up despite conditions that could hold you down. What such praise fails to see is the disappointment.

In his exquisite poem, "Digging," Seamus Heaney observes his own descent from men who labored. Of his father digging potatoes, he writes, "By God, the old man could handle a spade./Just like his old man." Against this raw strength, Heaney registers with melancholy humility, "I've no spade to follow men like them," and the poem concludes, "Between my finger and my thumb/The squat pen rests. I'll dig with it." The poem's beauty is its ambivalence, its reluctance to mark a generational shift from spade to pen as unambiguous progress. I long to wield both, and rue how often academic life would strip spades from those who have them. And that, more than anything else, is what I suspect betrays me as an imposter, though not in the anxious, normalized way.

Imposter syndrome rides on the perception, most fundamentally, that *one is getting away with something.* I struggle to grasp just why this sleight-of-hand ought to be counted a bad thing. I sometimes do still feel a fraud in academic environments, but neither do I mind it much. Indeed, taking a little pleasure in getting away with things is something I come by honestly – a family legacy, if you will.

When I was a child, my grandfather remarked that I had the Pentecost Eye. I took this as indication that I had special, perhaps even mystical, sight. Admittedly, I had not noticed any distinctive visual acuity or enjoyed spiritual visions, but this seemed of no account: if my grandfather noted I had the Eye, it must be something. And if it was named for the day that tongues of flame descended upon Jesus' disciples, it must surely be good and eventually prove worth having.

It turns out that the Pentecost Eye is but a droopy lid on one side, inherited from that branch of my family named Pentecost, some of the least holy people in the tree. One of these ancestors, Johnny Pentecost, lived on land that now sits on the edge of my family's present farm. Johnny was reputed to have come to the Ozarks after crossing the Mississippi while fleeing the law. A hard drinker and eager fighter, he told of having shot and killed a man one dark night, his explanation being that the man was after his horse. This at least was a version of the story, though it sounds like a tall tale told by one who liked to inspire fear. Still, whatever he got up to, Johnny bore knife scars on his back and those scars made it prudent to believe whatever confessions of past violent conduct he cared to make.

Johnny's homeplace on our farm was, strictly speaking, not *his* when he lived there. It was a patch of land he settled, never mind that it wasn't his. By the time the landowner got around to making something of this misappropriation, Johnny was dug in enough to make it more trouble to budge him than to leave him be. He was just not the sort easy to budge, and certainly not to budge without violence.

Johnny died long before I was born, and I expect we would have been much at odds had I known him. But in the too sterile life academia provides, I can't mind having inherited the Pentecost Eye. I find "imposter syndrome" best resisted by reminding myself that I am Johnny Pentecost's kin: none of my academic bona fides reassure me more than counting myself a squatter fiercely disinclined to budge. The land is not my own, yet here I abide, casting my drooping Eye upon the world.

12

Independence Day

"Is that Greg's?"

"I don't think that can be Greg's. Too far away and too far west. His will show, if they will, just there, across the Peak."

We can see fireworks to the west, coming from somewhere near that second ridge, a place well beyond our own, a place I've never been, though I sight it every time I look that way. It turns out that from our vantage point we can see the distant fireworks of people not known to us, the sky periodically alight and portioned out into what must be the farms of people doing as our people also do – firing up the sky out here where nothing but personal reticence bars blowing up or setting off whatever you might like.

I am sitting with my parents in the dark on the concrete slab that runs behind the old milk barn. The concrete provides stable footing for them, for they are both unsteady. We sit in lawn chairs, perched where years ago a daily wash of cow manure made its way from the barn's holding area down a slope to the lagoon. We've come here, in the dusk turning now to dark, to see the fireworks, if there are indeed any we can see. A hill, called Pike's Peak, stands between us and my cousin Greg's farm, and may well block the view. Greg reliably buys the ambitious fireworks, the ones that sail high but require some care lest you blow off some fingers using them. Even so, the Peak is in full foliage and just high enough that our view can only be uncertain.

In better times – really, in every year but this year of pandemic – we spend Independence Day on the other side of the Peak, at my cousin's farm. Our families have lived alongside, with the Peak our boundary, for more than one hundred years, though we only achieved kinship in the 1940s when my grandfather's sister married one of the sons of that farm. The magnificent fireworks on the Fourth are newer still than this. When my daughter was still small, our gathering together was for much tamer fare, the sort of thing achieved by handing over lighters, bottle rockets, and Black Cats to the children and hoping for the best. In the last dozen years or so, however, the Fourth has become a spectacle.

What began as a modest family gathering has grown to an event attended now by dozens, folks not just from the family but from surrounding farms, from the family's church, and from town. The potluck requires a tent and long tables that all comers then will burden with potato salads, chicken, and cakes decorated with red, white, and blue icings that will first ooze, then mingle, in the summer heat. Over all, my aunt and other ladies will wave empty paper plates in futile agitation against flies that will arrive in force. There is a fire blazing in a fire pit, hot dogs, marshmallows, and sharpened sticks for any who would like to roast their own. There are even sections of a sort, gatherings within the grander gathering. The older ones tend to fix their chairs and set in place, the middle aged to hover round the food or circulate, while the children nimbly hare off to some distance, the better to set off smoke bombs, make ash snakes, or shoot Roman candles away from older eyes or any who might scold them not to be so careless in how they aim the worst of what they have.

After most have had their fill of food will come a characteristic impatient aimlessness, that time when all want dark before it has come. This is the interregnum, when the eating ruled over by the women gives way, and we all abide in waiting for the men to start lighting up the works. One year, this time passed with a hayride taken on a flatbed round the field, but this was a joy altogether too mild to justify the labor it entailed – all round here know what's it's like to circumnavigate a pasture. I think the only ones who enjoyed it were my sister-in-law and me, and that was because we'd spiked our drinks. More lately, this time has passed disorganized, in talk or general idleness, though I have another cousin who will stand himself beneath a tree, there to read aloud the Declaration of Independence or the Constitution while some few souls unlucky enough to have sat near obligingly listen.

When dark at last comes on, Greg and some other men will gather far out in the field where they have parked a sizeable hay wagon heavy laden with combustible potential. Their voices, deep and often laughing, resonate across the distance till at last the first they light will burst above us. The sky out here is inky black, no city lights and naught but the fire to dull the contrast a good firework can make. The display is such to remind me why people ever started to pursue what should have counted as quixotic folly, why human ingenuity should ever have taken this particular turn and conceived a wish to explode colors in the sky. But in truth what I like best are the pops of human voice that intrude upon the general silence. Most watch with quiet awe, the way a people blowing up the sky should do, but there are always some who insert some verbal admiration. Better still are the sounds of those men way out in the field. They'll sometimes laugh, sometimes instruct, and sometimes gasp in ways that let all know they've just missed provoking some disaster. One year, they inadvertently set up beneath the power lines, and the extra frisson of alarm this caused joined with the marvel of it all – each burst of explosive light illuminating lines the fireworks just missed, the percussive gasps from all around more prevalent that year. This sense of tension, of comedy, of camaraderie in reckless effort is part of what we miss this year, there atop our own hill and set on the concrete, just we three, my parents and me. What tension we have found is all a sadder, melancholic sort, the kind that a pandemic will turn up.

There really shouldn't be a spectacle at all this year, not with the virus on the loose. But all of my more distant kin and the many who populate the place each year have determined that "life" should carry on. That life of the sort they thereby reference is already gone is a fact that none are inclined to grant. Facts are things one does not negotiate, so their talk instead intimates the stuff of struggles we might overcome or of battles we might win. Courage to go on with life, with our routines and with our ways, is what the moment calls for, or at least the call they claim to answer. So here we sit some near mile off, and I want to gasp, but with our loneliness.

We came out too soon, this much is plain. As impatient as the wait may be in an ordinary year, this wait is of a different order. It isn't just the stillness – the absence of the restive many, the lack of feral children armed with lighters. It's that we cannot even know if we will know when our kin have started off. We might not see a thing. The boundary between us may obscure it all and us be none the wiser, left to wait till such time as we at last just give it up as lost. Our people seem so far away, the Peak between us, and them on something I capitalize in my mind as The Other Side. The lonely thoughts crowd in fast with the coming dark.

We have been in isolation since mid-March, retreating from the wider world because my parents both are old and because my mother's doctor told us to in order to protect her. While we sometimes chafe against the bonds in just the way a sentient, social being would, we have managed mostly to endure. People who will live on farms and far from town have space to roam and are practiced in the several forms of solitude, so ours have surely been better than those taken in cities and by those used to crowded lands. The part to break my heart has been what others of our kin and neighbors do, their devotion to the usual and their resistance to aught that would be otherwise. We are the otherwise, the people now put on The Other Side. I would say that we're doing as needs must, they that we lack courage and, still worse, faith. This is what they in fact do say to my parents. That I am faithless is old news, but my parents stay the course with God and should, somehow, trust that He will do what my mother's immune system cannot, make it all come right if she should catch the virus. This mean theology of careless risk is now the mountain stood between us. My parents have been largely cast aside by the people they once counted as their own, but they are trying hard, set atop this cracked concrete, to deny it. These are thoughts I hide while I natter on in false cheer about what bird that was that we just heard or about the way my brother and I used to blow up plastic army men with Black Cats, the gravel lane left littered then with tiny green arms and legs. I wish I had to hand some sort of similar destruction I could carry out but keep this also to myself. This is not the first time we have felt bereft in the pandemic, but it surely is so far the worst.

With full dark on, we debate the wisdom of remaining. Just as my will to stay at last is broken, mercy comes with a chirp of my dad's phone. It's Greg texting from The Other Side to urge us to be ready. He's about to start the works and wants us not to miss it. His characteristic careless bonhomie should strike me with a sour note, I know. It will strike me as such later, but for now I am all and only the relief.

My mother has taken lately to saying that she does not mind the isolation of the pandemic. "It's just that," she falters, "I somedays wonder if there is still anyone else *out there*." For this day at least, she has a signal that there is. It's in the gasping pops of color now spiking against darkness, just there above the Peak.

13

Wasting my Fiftieth Year

I have come lately to suspect that I have largely wasted my fiftieth year. Here could commence a tedious recitation of the ways this might be so. We are in a pandemic, and I have found it paralyzing. My intellect stalls in even routine work; my body is a wreck from months of accumulated stress; my vocabulary is thin because I talk to few and rarely; and my will to make any of these matters otherwise abandoned me some months ago. These, I expect, are just the stuff of life as we must live it now, at least for those like me – those already bent by temperament to melancholy or to worry. I tried resistance for a time, tried capitulation, too. But what has come to aid me in a way I will try here to recount is fixing on my age. It came to me last week in some pleasant mental rearrangement, a sudden turning of the mental winds. To relate my insight now will be to talk as my grandmother would, to start at the beginning but veer off wide and far before I at last arrive at the thought that is my present therapy.

Unable to spend my time in the useful ways I used to do – writing, reading, thinking, doing manual labor out of doors – some time ago, I turned to more quixotic pursuits. This explains how I came to be down in the Ten Acre Patch sawing old fence boards by hand.

The Ten Acre Patch is a little used twelve-acre valley that lies on the farthest northeast corner of our farm. (Once he learned its proper measurement, my husband tried briefly to get us all to call it the Twelve Acre Patch, but we are a people committed more to our past than to accuracy.) I had gone to the Patch to find some different, less familiar place to be. I have many hides and haunts upon the farm where I retreat to be outside – a walnut grove beside the creek where the changing of the trees through seasons is enough to occupy my idled mind; a flat atop our hill from which I can survey the lake and, depending on the time of day, spy cranes or deer; a dip beneath a vast old oak beside the piles of rock my people built when they cleared the land for pasture. None of these would do that day because I had a purpose: I was there to saw up boards for scrap, then to paint on each a trouble that I have. Once I had assembled the troubles, I would set them all alight and make a woe fire so I could turn each trouble into ash. For this, the Ten Acre Patch appeared most impractical and so best. One wants a chore like this to be remarked by place and not just by the work, I thought, and good to loose the troubles into words where the farm around is at its loneliest and wild.

I hasten here to say I am not an especially superstitious sort. If troubles could be really burnt and thereby made to yield, I think we human beings would have sorted that out by now – perhaps the way we have our other garbage. We'd by now have civic pyres placed for common use wherever people dwell, or we'd have "trouble collectors" come to tote our burdens off and burn them for us. Yet even as I don't believe that troubles really yield to flame, I incline to think that some futile acts are still worth doing. There can be a clarifying relief in enacting longings we lack power to fulfill. It is sometimes a good to simply know just what it is you want, and torching troubles registers the wish for their destruction more potently than the wish alone will do. This, at least, is how I conceived the woe fire. Yet as often happens with too much I try to do, it did not take long to spy the gap that yawns wide between conception of a task and its material execution.

Sawing boards by hand in winter is both tedious and tiring, the work made worse when a truck tailgate is one's only sawhorse, worse still when one forgets to bring good gloves. On setting out, I was all energy, but this soon ebbed with the endless scratching of my saw. I also hadn't thought to count my troubles first or to think about how fine a parsing I would like to make. After all, if one will count one's troubles, one wants to have some system, a taxonomy and sense of scale.

It quickly comes to bother me to recognize how many troubles are related and represent a choice that I must make: summarize them into one or keep them separate, each with its own board? I could make one for my family's health or I could paint a board for each of our afflictions. Should I burn my husband's fractured spine, my father's crumbled ankles, and mother's broken wrist, or paint them all as one? And what of more elusive woes that work on me? How big a trouble should a trouble be to warrant being burnt? Does my intractable inertia count? I think I'd like it to because I'd dearly love to burn it. But with boards all sawn to near size, the boards become unseemly if my inertia sits on one and a global pandemic on another. These troubles should not be alike in scale – because they manifestly aren't – but on my boards they would be. Perhaps I could adjust for this with a third board for self-pity? These were the enervating thoughts that came to me belatedly, round about the time my wood scraps numbered thirty. It occurred to me that should I parse the troubles fine, I might keep sawing all my days and without cease. And then I also thought perhaps I should settle on but one – paint *THE WORLD* and grab the lighter fluid. Not one to solve a problem when I can dwell on it, I paused all work to lay in the truck bed and stare long at the sky. I was swiftly joined in this by my stray dog.

Dog has now followed me across the farm and home again each day for months. If I am on the farm, he is wherever I might go. (He is here now, nosing through some buckbrush while I type.) If I am home, he waits for me outside, nesting in a pile of leaves, stationed on the porch, or napping beside my truck so he can wake and join me if I leave. He is my guardian, too. When I emerge from the house, he makes haste to herd away the neighbor's cattle where they gather across the road, lest one unaccountably irritate or menace me.

I am here compelled to emphasize Dog's steady presence, his faithful daily constancy, in order to explain – I won't say *justify* – the way I talk to him sometimes. Most of our verbal interaction is just the prosaic stuff of dogs and people. I compliment his fine looks, his good character, and demand he leave those cows alone. But I also sometimes go a little farther, as I did that day while leaving off the sawing of my trouble boards. When he joined me in the truck bed for my rest, I idly scratched his head and this worked on me the way Dog often does. My gnarled thoughts about taxonomies of trouble gave way to restive impatience with my situation. The benevolent contentment of this dog, I find, will do this, will work some force that makes my inner life that bit too much to take. As I picked fresh burrs from his dense coat, I said, "Dog, I'm fifty years old and I'm in a pasture sawing boards so I can paint them with troubles just so I can burn them." This is when the waste of my year arrived in force.

When one has achieved fifty, one has a chance to frame all manner of one's doings with one's age, and fifty in particular lends a special jolt to what you do. At fifty – or so I have found it – one sits betwixt and between, the end of child rearing largely come but the end of one's parents an end one can foresee, if not yet already suffered. One is presumed competent, an adult, but also, so it seems, a bit too boring, fixed too firmly into place. At fifty, one is neither starting out nor finishing off. One should be mature but not yet truly old. One is still a bit resilient, but also somewhat stiff. All this in between, for me at least, means I have no natural place where I alight. I sometimes talk to Dog, but also wash the dishes.

When I was young, I thought that by the age of fifty my rough edges would have sanded down, that the tedium of things like chores would be a plight I'd just accept, as if resignation to dull duty were a gift the years alone would give me. *I am fifty years old and washing dishes again,* I now say daily. I find this well catches the prosaic tasks nigh unending at this age. At fifty, one has washed so many dishes and yet will have so many more to come. It's a kind of good to mark the spot, to own the Sisyphus of pots and pans you are. There will come a day for one's last dish, but it isn't yet, you get to say. And of course there's a bit of churlish in the dishes, in their ubiquity and repetition. Append all that with fifty and the tired, heavy self grows lighter in self-satire. One wants at fifty, after all, not to be undone by mundane dishes. Nor yet to be someone who simply takes all troubles in one's stride. In youth, I had assumed that fifty held the kind of wise that makes one staid, and I am relieved it isn't so. One sometimes wants to break a dish instead of wash it. One still gets up to things and, better still, can often do so freely. At ten, no one lets you start fires. At fifty, one can go slightly mad in ways no one can stop.

It is fifty's very in-betweenness that makes one neither comic nor quite tragic. Instead, I think and say to Dog, I believe I'm tragicomic. *I am fifty years old and explaining myself to a dog.* That is the magic bolt of fifty. Any sentence one can utter of oneself is much improved when prefaced with one's age. The age contains whole worlds of psychic revelation and relief. How, I think, have I been fifty for so many months and missed this?

Since that day, I have made all manner of frustration yield to this, to my inner narration of my life in the register of fifty. *I am fifty years old and . . .* I have discovered that appending this up front transforms most anything that follows. I have tried a bit to explain this to myself, to assess the source and nature of the transformation, but not too hard. Some tools are nicer to use than understand. Even so, I suspect it owes to something like the reason artists took up painting dogs playing poker – which is to say the incongruity. Dogs don't really play poker, so seeing them do it sets the world a little on a pleasing tilt. We like to witness things that do not really happen, creatures showing powers we don't think they ought to have. I expect that being fifty may be like this in some almost totalizing way – it is the age of incongruity. I have turned my age into a torch and made some troubles yield.

14

I Hope to Meet You There

When I am working on the farm, I think of the ancient Confucians more than I ought. In early Confucian tradition, it was understood that the body and life you have is a gift from your ancestors. This of course explains much where Confucian expectations of filial virtue are concerned. After all, having a life and body constitutes a significant sort of debt to discharge. Filial deference and gratitude seem a tricky business to me – hard to do when you're the younger, nice to get when you're the elder. It's a virtue I like more for my daughter than for myself. But it does seem right to me that there is something rather more collective than individual in the way that we are made.

Before there was ever any "me" to speak of, there were the people who combined to produce me. This is a truth told all over my body. I have my grandmother's neck (and should, by rights, add "alas" here since she would). I have my other grandmother's stout German *Hausfrau* frame. I have my father's bad feet, my mother's high cheekbones, my grandfather's twitchy legs, and blue eyes descended from a whole tribe of blue-eyed people. I even carry traces of those who died long before I lived, my Pentecost Eye being just one such trace. Sometimes

I fancy myself like a car cobbled together out of spare parts, a bit of him, a bit of her, and a bit of those from way back when. The Confucians would have me understand those parts as held on lease, features not quite *mine* since they are also and more fundamentally *ours*, my family's.

In early Chinese tradition, one of the filial duties was to return your body to the ancestors as they gave it, whole. Having been given the gift of one's bodily self, treating that self carefully was the least one could do – not for the filial any crimes that would in ancient China get you punished with an amputation, nor would they have a taste for tattoos or other voluntary and permanent alterations of one's physical, ancestral landscape. It's this bit of Confucian filiality that most snags my thoughts when working on the farm. For it seems to me that taking on the family farm, keeping *it* whole and in the family, is surely the most filial thing I've ever done, yet it is also and at once what surely condemns me to delivering on death a far more wrecked body than I would otherwise give back. I come to think in fact that my ancestors may be different than all the rest. I imagine them a special tribe of Ozark Confucians, their version of ancestral bequest the gift of a body and also the gift of a place to ruin it.

I have not worked the farm long, but already it tells upon my body. I no longer wonder why all those old men at the feedstore trudge in from the parking lot with a gait all stiff and stoved up. The trip into town does that to me too. Sitting in the truck after being upright and on one's feet laboring feels like rest until you try to walk again and find every joint protesting. Too many things the farm requires are like this – fine while you are at them but unmerciful if you stop. I have learned not to sit unless I'm ready for the aches and pains it will awaken. But worse than this are the inevitable injuries.

I broke my toe by dropping a telephone pole on it, the pole too heavy to lift but still I tried because it would have made a sturdy corner post for fencing. I mildly electrocuted myself trying to repair some busted wiring on an old workhorse cart. I have stumbled in the dark against a boulder in the rain. I laid that time in agony so long that when I finally stood, I could not tell if it was rain or blood I felt then running into my boot. As it happened, it was both, and the scar this left behind works as a reminder not to dash through rain in dark, but just get wet instead. Weather is a general challenge, as the chilblains in my hands can now attest. At least, these only bother me in the cold and mostly leave me be. More persistent and abiding are the pains I carry in my wrists. Too much wrangling this or that has left them permanently frail, though at least for this I can in part fault my academic job. For a life of lifting and a life of typing is a mix to make a mess of wrists. Worse still are my congenital vulnerabilities and my inability to guard against them well.

I am allergic to the stings of wasps, but wasps can't always be avoided. I've been stung while repairing the metal sheeting of the barn, a job that had to be done, the sting a peril necessary to court. I've been stung while moving timber, disrupting a nest where none by rights should be. I've been stung while brushhogging out in open pasture – that time a winged little bastard dealt me the blow just because I happened to pass by him. Each one induced fine swelling, for at swelling I excel. Most of these I just endure, but I have also learned that stings are not all alike. Some venom is more potent, some strikes more prolonged, some stingers imbued with an extra bit of irritating filth. The worst send me to Urgent Care for a round of steroids and a chance to awe the doctor. When last I went, she marveled, "What *is* all of this?" And then commenced a recitation of all she saw upon my arm: sunburn, of course, and sting, but also a lacework of punctures and deep lashes acquired in cutting thorn trees, along with two circular blistered burns from torching what I'd cut. (If a bit of ember lodges near your elbow, best not to close your arm in reflex from the heat, for this will make two matching burns, each a mirror of the other.) Oh, and poison ivy, she observed, you have a bit of poison ivy starting. This last alarms me in a way that little else will do. I have a talent for poison ivy rashing, and in this I seem unique. No others in the family seem as afflicted as I am. Or if they ever were, the affliction they have left me lodges forgotten far up the family tree. I'd like to blame the Pentecosts, for it was one of them who had me at my worst with it.

Farming is not all labor for productive purposes, at least as my family has always done it. My great-grandfather sacrificed a healthy grazing pasture just to make a ball field; one uncle periodically turned scraps of wood into sculptures and liked to hang stray skulls up in the trees; another built an entire replica frontier cabin, complete with outhouse. Sometimes, in short, we lark in follies, undertaking work where none is strictly needed. This family tendency explains why my brother and I conceived a wish a few years back to unearth the cistern dug by my great-great uncle, Johnny Pentecost, a cistern, as it happens, surrounded by an overgrowth of poison ivy.

Without a well, a cistern is a useful way to collect the water that you need, but once the need has passed, an open cistern becomes a peril. A cemented hole more than a dozen feet deep becomes a hazard when weeds and brush quickly come to cover where it sits. So, too, a hole that deep is not a thing to waste in a rocky land like ours where holes are dear because they're hard to dig, so mine have always used our disused cisterns as places to put what trash we cannot burn. This makes them archaeological in their way, their contents modest artifacts of what our family once had and used, and then discarded. This is how my brother and I developed a desire to excavate Johnny Pentecost's cistern. There are other cisterns on our land, but Johnny's personality entire was quite suggestive, him the sort one might expect to fill his cistern with the bones of enemies, or at least some fine old bottles, once he'd drunk them dry.

Johnny Pentecost was one of the family's rougher sorts. His tendency to fight upon most any provocation and a corresponding need to flee the law is what brought him here. But by the time he dug that cistern we would excavate, his days of fighting, if not yet of his drinking, were likely then behind him. In age, he'd settled into milder forms of mischief, squatting on land that wasn't his and getting what he could in what crooked ways he found ready then to hand. When government aid came to the Ozarks during the Depression, old Johnny was known to be creative in counting what livestock were his. The first time the government agent showed up to take a head count of Johnny's stock, he had all his own there for the counting. When Johnny found out that fewer stock would bring in greater aid, he concealed some of his for the next counting. A little money on the dole was good, more money on the dole was better, and no need to be over-precise in measuring what constitutes one's state of want. Despite all of this, Johnny was not wholly without religion. By his own account, he had read the Bible seventeen times, but he avowed that he "just couldn't live it." I've always felt a special affinity for Johnny Pentecost, and not only because I have the Pentecost Eye. I haven't read the Bible seventeen times, but I can't live it either.

In preparation for our excavation, my uncle mowed all that sat around Johnny's cistern. In this, he cut the poison ivy there, but don't mistake that for a good. It meant we did not see it and cut poison ivy leaves stubs raw and wet, its irritating oils uncontained and oozing freely. In the days that followed, my brother and I dug out the earth that covered the cistern and in the process bathed ourselves in oil. By the time we reached the bottom of the cistern and knew that Johnny left us naught, the ivy had already done its worst.

On me, the poison ivy worked like plague, and I was left a month entire to suffer, my body a contamination of itching and the bone-deep aches that itching made. Any touch of sun or heat was unbearable. I laid indoors all daylight hours, making a tormented study of the rafters in my room. Neither could I sleep, not just for the itching but for the wakefulness so many steroids will induce. Restless every night, I took to driving through the dark just to feel the air upon my skin. When I could drive no more, I'd finally park my truck in a broken little town nearby – the town as desolate as me, its buildings mostly hollowed husks, its hundred souls asleep. Too tired to drive on and naught else to do, I made a study of the feral cat that nightly stalks those streets. It was in the distortion of this time that thoughts of my filial predicament most began to rise in me.

Awake while others slept, my skin a hair shirt I could not remove, I thought more provokingly of bodies than anyone ought to do. I assigned to Johnny Pentecost a malevolent haunting nature. I imagined his ancestral Eye cast upon my sleepless, itching own, and his would glint with mocking laughter. Not for him unnecessary labor undertaken on a lark. And so not for him any pity for my plight. He came to feature in my mind as one who would make sport of others' pain, especially such a self-inflicted, foolish kind. If you're dumb enough to dig for treasure in the cistern of a welfare cheat and squatter, you deserve whatever tax in pain you later have to pay. We were not so alike after all, me and that vengeful dead sadist. Compelled to look for pity elsewhere, I'd find it in myself.

Self-indulgent and dramatic in my misery, my mind would travel the dark road back toward home even as I sat parked on the lonely street. Perhaps, I thought, I will go to the graveyard and just lay now upon my grave. I could cast my tortured body down and let the ancestors have it back, blistered and early. Perhaps I would hurl curses all the while and reproach them for what they left me. More likely, I would hope they'd deal me a bit of sympathy and take me into their worn out, tired company. These ancestors knew both work and what it meant to stop. I wagered none of them liked Johnny either. Together we might rest atop that rocky hill, and from its height we could in utter idleness just watch the farm go wild. Its pastures and forests would soon be overtaken by all we had each, in our turn, tried so hard to resist: thorn tree, wild rose, thistle, buckbrush, knapweed, Johnson grass, and gooseberry, relentless problems all. The landscape would finally and at long last be left alone to tend the ways it wants to tend, ourselves free but to bear witness and without the fight, the way one can with troubles not one's own. But in the prospect of such imagined and complete relief, my thoughts would turn, as distorted thoughts will do, and I would fancifully imagine the farm entire in a singular compression of its past and populated all at once by all whom it had injured.

Babies died there, their mother, my great-grandmother, a bit more dimmed each time in these accumulated sorrows. In the farmhouse bedroom, my grandparents had sat awake when one of theirs had almost died. Somewhere along the lane, my mother lost a toe when she was only tiny – never for her any sandals that would betray the fact. Then there is the barn where many slowly wrecked their hands in years of milking. And out beyond the barn stands ground that carried the current of lightning through my grandfather, and this had happened more than once. Somewhere runs a stretch of fence near which he accidentally opened his own leg with an ax. One hillside had my uncle flip the tractor and dive away to merely bruise before it crushed him, a tale he told me once in caution. And up another hill stands the gate where that uncle one night shot himself and died, that spot of concentrated pain the greatest of them all by far. Some places on the farm are worse than others, but I did then come to expect that over all of it, the place entire, stretched generations of our aches and pains: whole crowds of cuts, punctures, stings, burns, bruises, fractures, entire fields of wounds and, sometimes, shattered hearts. I would then wonder where on the farm I might find a place where none of mine had sometime hurt. I doubt such a spot exists.

To imagine all that hurt and all at once is quite the trick, a transformation of the place. Maybe this is, by better rights, the real ancestral landscape, the great collective injured, aching body, the place itself but one accumulated howl of agonies unending. Unless of course some one of us should make an end and shuffle off that land of sorrows, just call it quits: If the landscape is our pain, it's a pain we could sell off at auction. I marveled then that none had done it, at how all had held it fast. In some romantic cast of mind, this might bespeak a familial resolve, ourselves made noble in endurance. But that is not my cast of mind as I sit wakeful through the nights unending, made half mad with itching. I expect instead not one of us can at last and finally begrudge what it will do to us, for we all are snared by our collective suffering. Each individual body will give and give because those others gave theirs first. And then, but only then, when one body is exhausted, the next generation will lay what's left among the rest, the bones themselves absorbed along with all the others. To keep my body whole would be, I can't help but think, to make it also lonely.

I never could get past this, parked and itching there upon the quiet street. My thoughts would stall on just what it could mean, for me and also for all of us, both the living and the dead. Soon enough the feral cat would grow restive, a sign of dawn's approach. He wants the mourning doves now stirring in the growing light. They have made a dovecote for themselves in an empty building, that refuge for the doves also a treasure for the cat. He wants to kill those doves, but they are also many. Because I could not stand the coming light, I'd point my Eye homeward and leave before what happened next.

15

Slipping the Net

In addition to being a philosophy professor, I am also an occasional graveyard keeper – though after both of these roles, I feel compelled to add "of a sort." Our graveyard is too modest really to need a keeper. It's just above an acre, set upon a hill and nestled all round by working farmland. In truth, its keepers have historically been many and, in that way, really none at all. The graves have just been tended by whichever of the living had the mind and will to do it. The vagaries of chance and mortality being what they are, sometimes there are no keepers because the keepers died. Lately, though, the graveyard has had many. This owes in part to recent losses. Put someone new in there, and this will generate in those still left a resolve to keep all tidy. That has been the usual way of the place, the ebbing and flowing of loss and survival come in like tides and then recede until fresh loss will raise the waters once again.

More than a decade ago, our graveyard went the way of most things and acquired a bureaucracy – though here again, it is only "of a sort." A land dispute brought this change on, for a woman who owned some of the abutting acreage began to make noises suggesting that her territories took in the graveyard too. She spoke as if she owned the land in which our dead are laid and, given how she managed what was hers, noises about ownership worked like an alarm. My mother and some other kin made haste to discover what provisions exist in law or policy to protect a place where dead are kept. Whatever its many shortcomings, the law was here enough, but in consequence of all of this, the graveyard now is registered and has keepers made official, a "board" consisting of my mother, an uncle, and a cousin once removed. My mother was, on its inception, the board's real force. She had the graveyard surveyed and mapped.

The map is just the style that one would want for such a thing. It is no scrap, but of a size that one must clear away the table when one wants to spread it out, a vast expanse of detailed markings. It shows the longitude and latitude, recording just where on the globe of earth entire our dead rest. The oldest graves are haphazardly arranged, their locations answerable to a logic I imagine was most immediate, the graves selected with the urgency of fresh griefs and the need for burial, their locations chosen for a view, the prospect of a shading oak, or their proximity to others. This seems clear at least in some cases. My grandfather's infant sister is flanked by kin who long outlived her. Little Elizabeth lived but briefly, her grave for decades marked only by a plain rock, yet she spends eternity nestled next to her own grandmother, her great-grandmother, and an uncle. These graves and all of the older others are sketched across our map just as they lie in life, at angles or in the clumsy clusters that I hope brought comfort to those who laid them there. The surveyor's map traces out small rectangles to register the spot for each, the shapes like little coffins on the page.

The most significant intervention emerging from the formal survey of our graveyard was that the land entire was mapped for future dead. A rational plotting of where new graves should go was made, the spaces measured, and the gaps between them too. To envision the place full, as the surveyor must have done, is to conceive a landscape ordered into rows and grids, walkways passing in between. In short, it would look the way most graveyards do – no more setting some at angles or some facing west while others look east. Our newest dead will also be our tidiest.

As is true of most maps, this one has a crisp clarity that only the simplification needed for abstraction can give. It is the effort to connect the paper map's plotting to the land itself that had me down on hands and knees, crawling over graveyard earth in search of signs. The surveyor sunk metal spikes, topped each with a round metal disk, to indicate where ordered plot corners go – once you find a corner pin, measurement from there can help identify the proper place and shape a new grave should take. As breadcrumbs left to show the way, they aren't much and by now are covered over, if not themselves just buried. Knowing this, when I went in search of pins, I brought along a measure wheel, tape measure, and bright pink flags and paint. A neighbor's father is poorly, his prognosis for death quite soon. It was my job to find and mark some few of the empty plots alongside a grand tree so his son can choose a place for when the fast-coming time arrives. The board members are now too old for this work and, in my fifties, I count as young enough to do it.

Even with the map in hand, I quickly abandoned as hopeless seeking out the pins that mark the corners of sets of empty graves. I started with graves already and more lately filled. These postdate the surveyor's work and so were laid along the patterns that our map describes, and their shapes are clear, their corners known. I decided to start with the newest grave nearest the grand oak, the place where my sister-in-law is buried. Maribeth's grave was once mine. When she died, altogether too young, my brother hadn't yet selected a spot to call their own, but I had one. Garret and I had on some anniversary then lately passed given each other graves, laying out the $25 that each would cost and selecting from the map a site where we would be alongside in death as we so often are in life. We never know what to give each other for an anniversary, but this seemed fit enough. Thus it was that when my sister-in-law died with no spot already set for her, we gave over our graves, one for my sister-in-law in this sad urgency and one for my brother (let it be long before he needs it). Maribeth is now buried just north of my cousin's wife, and that, too, seemed apt and fitting. Both women once were fierce, both were bested by a cancer that would early kill them. I here digress a bit, or maybe not. Marking graves in a family graveyard means marking too one's memory. It is personal. Graves are never only graves but more akin to monuments to pains that never fully pass. With Maribeth's more recent grave, I reasoned, I should be able to measure out the proper distances to find the empty spots, locate there a corner pin and then measure out and mark the many more empty spaces that our graveyard keeps in wait. However sensible this sounds, it did not really work.

If one is hunting a metal disk no bigger than a quarter and one at least grown over with fescue, if not submerged in soil, one needs more than just to know *about* where it should be. Lines of measurement walked out with a measure wheel can yet angle off or fail in straightness, or at least this is what I suppose mine did. This is how I ended up in a crawl, hoping my prodding fingers sunk in soil could find what my eyes and measuring could not. I found one after about ten minutes spent on hands and knees. In triumph, I clawed away the soil round it, sunk a tiny pink flag and spray-painted the pin orange for good measure. Then my trouble really started.

Because each plotted set of four graves will have two pins – some at the set's head, some oddly at the feet – I should have been able to pace out just where the next pin sat. I mentally recited my mapped truths: Each grave is five feet wide and ten feet long; each cluster of four graves is then surrounded by a five foot gap before another cluster then begins. With one pin found, then, I could either pace out the twenty feet to find its match and identify one clear boundary for a set of graves, or I could head west instead, tracing out five feet for the gap between, and then the ten more for the next set just above it. In the end, I tried both, and both to no avail. I cycled through a series of gestures – first pacing with the measure wheel, then crawling on the ground to poke in earth; extending out the tape measure in the hopes of straighter lines, then crawling once again to seek a pin. I discovered heaps of stones this way, unearthing each preceded by vain hopes that the hard shape my fingers found would be a pin, hopes that would be dashed by yet another rock. I began to doubt whether maps and surveys really are the boon that they might seem. I wondered if it would be better just to dowse a spot and call it done. I had tried this once before.

The local PBS channel used to run a series on Ozark history and I saw one program that featured talk of graveyards and of local folkways. There is a process, once presumably most common, for assessing whether a bit of land is free of grave, for knowing whether where you stand conceals some long ago forgotten dead. Called "grave dowsing," the practice involves using wires that, so the expectation goes, will twitch to indicate when earth is occupied. Given that we are a modern people, the technique now includes plastic straws and wire hangers. One cuts a wire hanger into two pieces, each piece then bent and shaped to make a right angle. One end of each wire angle is then placed inside a length of plastic straw. To dowse the grave, you then need to grasp a straw in each hand, with the wires in one's hands free inside the straw to turn as they will, and the wires bent at angle pointing forward. Holding the straw-enclosed stems, you then pace out the space that you would like to check. If the ground beneath your feet contains a corpse, the wires will spin inward and cross; if they do not, the ground is clear. In effect, the process is just like dowsing for water, but for bodies – a bit of divination turned to grimmer purpose.

My turn at dowsing came one idle day some years ago, around the time that Garret and I selected our second pair of graves. I have my doubts about the reliability and soundness of this practice, to be sure – the same doubt I hold about Ouija boards or any other magic business where a body can convulse its will upon the alleged art. Still, if one will call a grave one's own while living and if it sits in land where unmarked graves are said to be, it makes a kind of prudent sense to try some dowsing just in case. I'd hate for mine to dig to bury me and find old bones where they would aim to put me. That was how I reasoned then. I cannot help but here acknowledge that my compatriots in the profession of philosophy might dispute the use of "reasoned" in this way. Can one really *reason* oneself into a superstitious practice unsupported by any empirical evidence? In addition to scarring up my body some, farming has also compromised my use of "reason" – not exactly reason itself, perhaps, but at least the word. Sometimes when I "reason," I just "reckon." The Chinese poet Tao Yuanming worked for decades as a scholar in a city, then at last retreated to a farmstead. Of his time in scholarship, he wrote, "By mistake I fell into a dusty net, and all of a sudden thirty years had passed." I think of him whenever I am called to reckon, and reckon I can sometimes slip the net.

When I dowsed my new grave, the wires did not spin and cross. The space where I will spend that last rest is empty, at least so far as divination can reveal. For years after, I kept my plastic straw and wire hanger gear on the dashboard of my truck. I'd tossed them there in carelessness when done, and then just decided that you never know and left them there. When that ratty truck gave up the ghost, my dowsing gear then got carried off inside the truck when I sold it up for scrap. Standing in the graveyard with only the gear of precise measurement and our too exacting map, I regretted the loss of those wires and straws. Surely anyone wanting a new grave wants most one that is just empty, whatever this later age's vain precision in marking spots. Could we not abandon this new way and simply seek out some stretch of earth so far unoccupied, rigid rows and sets be damned? These are the thoughts that passed as I knelt with my head upon the grass and prayed to a god I don't believe in to give me just one more pin. But that mood, like most moods, at last lifted.

Since I took up my family's farm, I have grown accustomed to frustration. There is so much in the material world that will not yield to my wishes, so much that it affords in opposition to my plans. Some frustrations yield as one gets better skilled – since gravel roads make a mess of tires, I can now have one off and changed in just a few minutes – but some, and likely more than merely some, do not. When the hard parts of the world most stubbornly refuse to yield to me, I have learned to leave off fighting fate to let the helplessness wash over me. Small problems then recede from my attention and I tarry on larger confusions. What am I doing here? Or, how did I get here? These are not questions of despair but of an arresting relief. The bland and altogether tamed order of my life is not yet just all there is. To be sure, I often have to cloak myself in the languages and signs of a learned scholar, and speak with a "reason" that others of that kind can find familiar. But somehow the wildness of life has also brought me here, to crawling upon graves. Only one of these provides the leavening indignity that turns life into pleasure.

Frustration makes so many of us foolish. I am trying instead to turn my own to some account, to sacralize not will but its absurdities. So, after more than three hours poking grass upon my hands and knees, I cast myself most truly to the earth, not as I would measure it, but as it is. I take a rest upon the ground and splay myself across some empty grave plots of a number I cannot determine. Am I stretched across one or many? No one here can say. The surveyor might be able to tell, but I am not he. I am just a creature of bent wishes and dirty fingernails, prone across the land. The branches of that grand oak do break up the sky in such a remarkable way. There are no straight lines up there, cutting up the view. It is all and only crookedness.

I eventually raise myself again to my feet, dust myself off, and drive into town to buy a metal detector.

16

The Armor of God

My grandma Ruby's hair was a stern, tight, and seemingly impenetrable helmet. It sat atop her high forehead, apparently impervious to insults from weather, wind, or the pressures of her pillow in sleep. Her hair bespoke resolution, an unwillingness to bow before the messes to which others carelessly submit. Beyond her weekly trip to the beauty shop for a set, she did little with it. She didn't have to. The most she ever did was take to it with a little metal pick. A few judicious lifts with the pick could restore its height or shape if some malignant force briefly brought it low. Her hair was not easily or long discouraged. It stayed as was and as ever would be, at least it seemed so when I was a child. In church, when the preacher solemnly invoked our need to "put on the whole armor of God," it was Ruby's hair to which my thoughts would turn. My grandmother had the hair of a warrior: fierce, proud, and defiantly unbowed by ordinary mortal influences. In hindsight, that seems right and more than justifies the expense of a weekly set in hard times.

The farm ledgers from even the poorest years in my grandparents' early married life invariably contain an entry labeled simply "Hair" and the expense was, relative to others undertaken, extraordinary, both in its amount and the regularity with which it was spent. With three children and all manner of stock to feed, the farm ledgers trace out a life with clothes sewn at home from fabric bought cheap and every nickel accounted for. Still, however stretched taut, the income reached, always, to Hair. This might suggest some vanity or waste, but I cannot think it so.

What we will count essential sometimes needs to own that what matters most is spirit, and Ruby's hair was hers. Armored in her stiff, unbending curls, she could take on whatever came, and to spend a bit on that would be a cost worth paying. I expect the symbolic force of Ruby's hair was achieved most by what it wasn't. It was not dirty, low, chaotic, poor, or careless – traits one and all her upbringing would predict as hers. Ruby's hair was just the most conspicuous of her features to announce that here was order, here was dignity, here was a person fearsome and of substance. Most basically, a person with her hair was a person who could pay to have a set. More ambitiously, a person with hair so unflinchingly well ordered would be a formidable force against which any manner of human folly or even fate itself would have to reckon. More regrettably, a person with her hair would not have a grandchild with hair like mine.

Not for Ruby the warrior's dress that would be hers alone. She meant to conscript me too, and a more unwilling, reluctant soldier the world had never seen. My careless, untended adult hair was long foretold by the hair I had in childhood. The hair itself was inoffensive and banal – fine strands of brown that, because they would not curl, would also freely take a comb. The trouble was my tendency to hang it in my face. My hair would hide what Ruby called my "nice blue eyes." And, too, my ponytails were never kempt or tidy. I was, in short, a messy, shaggy sort of kid, and more than once Ruby menaced me with threats of scissors. She never cut my hair but professed the wish most often. My abiding sense when she turned her gaze on me was that her fingers fairly tingled with the wanting. My teenage years were worse than even this.

I came into my teenage years during the 1980s, a period for human hair diabolically designed to test the will of a woman like Ruby. Over the course of that decade, I had all the worst it had to offer: A period of frizzy perms that makes me wince in recollection, hair teased into a high nest of tangles held together by an injudicious use of hairspray sold in cans as big as aqualungs, and, worst of all, asymmetrical cuts that had half shorn too short and the other half drooping long across my face. Each visit to the farm, I showed up with some fresh hell of hair. I could be a trial upon Ruby's nerves just by sitting at the supper table. She would mostly forbear daily comment, but taking me to church would bring on crisp advice delivered in tones of high exasperation. "Couldn't you just . . . ," "You would look so pretty if . . . ," "Why don't you . . . ?" The only mercy in it all was that it would not last. My more consistent inertia would reassert itself at last. I didn't have it in me to spend the time my own hair took to keep it looking big or frizzy or uneven. Having seen the worst that I could do with hair, Ruby gave up any fight against mere shabbiness. It was only in her last years that I found some will of my own, discovering in myself an inheritance of her fierce impulse to care for Hair.

Ruby spent longer dying than she liked. Or, rather, she was convinced both that she was dying and that she would prefer to die long before she did. She was not by nature or temperament inclined to see her life through a glass darkly and did not take leaving life lightly. Rather, in aging, she simply evinced what she ever had, the unconflicted clarity of her own displeasures. What she did not like, she announced plainly, to herself and often to others. And she did not care for aging and failing health. It was not simply the pain, though there was more than enough of that, but the diminishing of her considerable dignity. Hers had been a fierce and powerful life. At her life's end, though, her struggles, like herself, all seemed to be reduced.

Born to slay the foes of chaos and disorder with fierce competence and sharp command, at the end she met the grinding adversaries of aging, the ones that make it hard to dress and eat, hard to think straight or, at root, to want to live at all. This all told upon her hair.

When Ruby reached her eighties, her hair began alarmingly to gentle, its well-armored severity giving way to wispy, cottony curls soft to the touch. Some days the back of her head would wear the mark of her pillow, the curls crushed and defeated against her skull. Most days she would not pick it back to lift and life. Without the will or spirit to marshal her curls back into battle formation, she would but leave them lay in all of their considerable discouragement. To be clear, her hair did not become a mess. It simply became what hair most often is yet never was for her, a thing unruly that will succumb to wilting and collapsing – a thing affected by fate. My grandfather could not accept this.

My grandfather never much cared about his own hair, but he did suffer it once to be conscripted into an armor Ruby fashioned. When I married Garret, my grandmother worried about how she and my grandfather would be perceived by Garret's people, people from New England who had both money and a kind of class and culture. My grandfather's usual hair was always the same short cut one sees in movies from the 1940s, brushed back along the sides and top. He was always handsome with it too, but for our wedding, Grandma had him wear his hair in bangs combed down upon his forehead. Men who farm wear caps and this tells upon their faces, browned jaws fade to pale foreheads – Ruby wanted my grandfather wearing bangs to hide his farmer's tan line. His hairdo at our wedding was a marvel, the bangs that hid his cap line making him vaguely ridiculous. The day after our wedding, he went back to wearing it, and not caring about it, the way he always had. But when in the injuries of aging, Ruby set down caring about her own hair, he picked up caring for her.

So long as he could drive, my grandfather never let go taking Grandma to town "to Hair." Going "to Hair" was our collective shorthand for Grandma's weekly appointment at the beauty shop to get her set put in, a process that involved a shampoo, a modest trim, a lot of fearsome-looking curlers, and a real helmet – the drier helmet that would decisively weld the armor of her curls in place. She did not often want to go, but Grandpa would gently and stubbornly cajole her into it. When his own health at last lost him his driver's license, he conscripted others to this task, and I was one. I quickly came to see why even as he could surrender much to aging and decline, he would not give up her trips to Hair.

Taking Grandma to Hair could be a trial. She was often frail and tired, and not inclined to see the point. Her physical frailties meant taking great care that she could go from house to car, from car to beauty shop, without a stumble. The frailties of her spirit often meant riding into town in sullen silence. But the process itself was like a resurrection, the dryer helmet lifted like a stone rolled from the tomb, and Grandma would emerge fearsome, fierce – Herself. Once fitted out again in her familiar armor, some long-trained warrior's instinct would reassert itself.

Trips home from Hair were journeys back in time to that world where she was not just sharp but garrulous with it, her commentary on all she saw at once biting and comically sardonic. Here once again was the woman who would tell small children that she'd like "to slap you to sleep and then slap you for sleeping." And here she was unbowed by mortal frailties, ready to draw these too into sightline of her verbal fire. Pretending blindness, she'd declare in great disgust, "This town has changed so much that I'm sure if I weren't blind and could actually see it, I would not even recognize it." This was Ruby as was, pinching judgment coupled with vigorous self-satirizing wit. She would announce her displeasures but remark too upon the folly of displeasure. Not all that fate would give us, she seemed to intimate, deserves our battle dress, but so long as we are indeed well armored, we might make a sharpish bit of sport, of the world and of ourselves. I took to driving her through McDonald's to buy her orange Hi-C, just for the delight of hearing her caustically declare that it tasted so good that a person could well mistake it for fresh squeezed.

Ruby's hair had been her armor; for us it came to be a battle flag. Sometimes grief can make you over into someone else's standard-bearer, heading up a charge that's doomed but that you take on anyway. Not all soldiers heading for defeat will give up easily. But defeat still comes; even resurrections cannot last. Eventually, the trips to Hair became more than she could bear, and Ruby's last months passed unprotected.

The night that Ruby died, I was on the highway hastening toward the farm. The call had gone out late that afternoon that any who could get by to see her should come on, that she was unlikely to last. I was just one of several on the road that night, the farmhouse and her bedroom pulling us all inward. I had not yet then succumbed to owning a cell phone, so I just drove as fast as I dared and in ignorance of whether I still had a grandmother. Somewhere about two hours out, where the roads grow darkest and towns are scarce, I did not. But I wouldn't know that till I got to the farm and saw my mother standing on the porch. There's no good reason to stand on a porch after midnight if your own mother is at work dying, so at least my mother did not need to give the news out loud. Ruby was then still at home. My grandfather would keep her there till morning so that we, her family, could set with her in the old way.

The dead are not like the living, but neither are they wholly unlike. When I set beside my grandmother that night, I wanted much I will not here relate, I was unhappy with much I will not here write. Her hair was then in full defeat, its pale wisps disordered where they were not flattened by her pillow. I tried to fix it with my fingers, to tidy her a bit, but as her hair in life refused to yield to chaos, her hair in death refused to yield to me. My grandfather must have understood the way that her wilted, wild hair was totemic of a grief that could go wild and wilt us all. Or maybe he just knew that hair like Ruby's, so long in the fight, deserved a warrior's final rest. He called the beauty shop one last time. When the undertakers took Ruby to the funeral home in town, she would be met by her hairdresser.

At the visitation, I stood for a time with my grandpa by the coffin, one hand gripped tight around the back of his belt because he seemed like to topple. He stood there as an ancient, loyal sentry would, or as just a husband who has been with a woman for 67 years and can't work out how, at this late date, to part. His hair that sorry day was as it always was, and so was mine – his revealed his cap line, mine was frayed and messy – but still we laid her down as she had lived, well armored for the grave.

17

Ways to Kill a Groundhog

The young man my father hired to help out with chores he can no longer handle is setting out to mow. He steers our large mower toward the barn lot, his posture relaxed but his rifle at the ready, resting long across his lap. We have acquired our own sharpshooter. Since he shares a name with my own husband, we call him Young Garrett. (My Garret I only call just that – "My Garret" – not wanting (yet at least) to style him "Old.") Young Garrett is a prize-winning trap shooter and, at but seventeen, a startlingly accomplished naturalist. We have set him armed upon the place in hopes that he can aid with our late trouble. We are under siege by groundhogs.

For a peaceful decade, we had hosted at least one groundhog, as evidenced by the longstanding hole just under the wall of the milk barn. But about four years ago, we noticed holes beginning to appear inside the old calf barn and underneath the shop. None of this was good or acceptable – groundhogs can be quite destructive – yet it likewise seemed a kind of tolerable, the sort of problem one puts off and off, postponed for an imagined sometime coming day when nothing else wants one's attention more. But what began at slow and steady pace has found a sudden increase. We have holes now in the dozens, groundhogs in a number I hesitate to guess. So overrun has our area become that even our gentle, vegan neighbor confessed she wanted to buy a gun and learn to shoot. It was then that I belatedly faced up to our trouble and set myself to fix it.

I am not a natural at the bits of farming that set one at war with other creatures. I prefer to coexist whenever we can manage it. All the same, one doesn't get to live that way – not when, say, mating skunks take up residence under the bedroom or pack rats try to winter over under the hood of our best truck. Even so, I try to keep my heart tender. I have a skunk trap that will sometimes work. It's designed to lure the creature into a long tube, there to hold it where its noxious tail can't raise. What happens next is a matter of some ambiguity, a choice left to the trapper. I don't drown them as some would but instead take them to church. If you will relocate a skunk, you need to take it far, too far to make its way in some return. So that is what I do. There is a native stone church some nine miles down our dirt road, the church long ago abandoned and left empty. It's nestled up a hill by woods that I would like, were I a skunk. So I take my skunks there. (It helps to have a building I can hide behind when time comes to open up and release them – the drive to church does tend to make them irritable.) Like the skunks, the groundhogs cannot be left to live with us, lest the hordes now upon us really do undermine a barn or have us breaking axles or ankles across their many holes.

My efforts in groundhog control began in modest ways. Groundhogs do not like foul smells, and so stinking up their territories seemed a good first step to take. Coyote urine was far too costly, so I settled on vinegar for my stink, bathing the holes under a barn daily. But it turns out that if you will stink up a groundhog's hole, she'll just dig another entrance to her tunnel. So I put my vinegar away and started setting out a trap.

My groundhog trap is a humane sort, a welded wire cage that closes behind a creature once it steps on a metal plate to retrieve the bait. For days, I set that trap with cantaloupe and waited, all to no avail. Our finest apple tree was then producing, and I speculate that the groundhogs had no need of store-bought melon when we had a grassy patch of glorious windfall regularly on offer. This is not to say that the trap failed entirely to work, for work and overtime it did. Within two weeks I had caught three possums, one armadillo, and five raccoons. The possums I would just release, for they eat ticks and we really like them for it. I took the armadillo off to our far woods, hoping he would not come back, but by then not caring overmuch about a one such as himself. Because they are so crafty and so diabolical, the raccoons I took out to that church. They arrived in my traps in such quick succession that I began to tire of the long drive each would require. I consoled myself with speculative imaginings about their later fates. I fancied them out there forming a new religion, one that has as origin myth a Great Relocation. Raccoons only travel on their feet, but these would with their feet confined still end up somewhere new – surely a fate most radical and peculiar, if one is a raccoon. Each alone might think he was gone slightly mad, but together their common story of the Relocation would start to seem like more. It could be a tale to circulate for generations about how they started out in one place and then – somehow, no one can say for sure – they ended up in another, all together and at church. Such is the stuff of which myths could readily be made. But none of this was consolation for my elusive groundhogs.

As is the way with much out here upon our farm, one sometimes has to give up searching in the predictable places for solutions. What the internet or extension office can't tell you, someone out here might. So I started talking of our groundhogs whenever circumstance gave me the chance. This is how I began to assemble a catalog of ways to get rid of groundhogs.

The most straightforward way to rid oneself of groundhogs is to kill them, and the most straightforward way to kill a groundhog is naturally to shoot it, but unless one will live armed, it is a solution not well matched to circumstance. One needs a gun just when chance puts a hog across your path, and since I wasn't going to carry constantly, this was not a remedy to work. Since all around are alert to just this trouble, most of the local solutions involve strategies for getting groundhogs to appear. One neighbor suggested strings of Black Cats, those percussive small fireworks that in clusters can make quite a chaos. Just light and toss those in the hole, he said, and wait there with my gun: When the noise sends the groundhogs out, have your rifle at the ready. Even if I could reconcile myself to this, it didn't seem for me too prudent. I am not a graceful person, a deficit a loaded gun could only complicate. So, too, I recalled my grandfather's talk of "some old fella" who tried to shoot an armadillo and instead shot his own trailer. The bullet ricocheted from there to hit his dog right in the eye. I too much like my dog and his fine eyes to try to aim my rifle amidst a haze of fireworks.

One of my father's friends offered up flooding as a better solution than a gun. Block up any exits, then just run the hose down in a hole and let the water rip till naught inside could well survive. This had its appeal, but still I foresaw problems. While my hose is long, the groundhogs don't take care to only dig within its reach. The holes my hose can get are also those beneath our barns, and I don't trust our now aged structures to withstand flooding underneath. I could well conceive a watery grave full of groundhogs and a sunken barn atop. Similar reservations had me balking at what a guy down at the feedstore promised worked a trick. He, too, suggested fluid down the hole but gas instead of water. "Just run some fuel down in those holes," he said with energy that made me uneasy, "then light 'em up!" Having rejected the elements of both water and fire, air presented as another possibility when another feedstore fellow suggested I gas the creatures out: Connect a hose from the exhaust of the truck down into a hole and run the engine till a toxic excess of emissions poisons any groundhogs luckless enough to be at home. Here, too, a little gunfire might be joined with fumes, as I could shoot any coughing hogs that emerge to flee a death by poisoned air. I had no ready, clear objection to this approach – no sense that with it I might destroy more than I meant. Yet still I could not like it, and disliked it with an unsettling but utter certainty that I would never try it. This failure to find a strategy that I could bear or trust is how we came to hire our young gunslinger.

Young Garrett is the best shot for miles around, but even he is struggling. He has succeeded where I did not, his tally of groundhogs killed now at three. He is always armed, but on the whole his efforts so far have proven much like mine, with lots of accidental catches in the mix, though his catches meet an end far grimmer than mine did. After one especially noisy afternoon of gunfire coming from the barn lot, Young Garrett came in to report that while he added no more hogs to his existing tally, he had managed still to shoot one snake, one snapping turtle, and two mice. (He is indeed a good enough shot to hit a mouse.) That day, he came in talking like I used to do, speculating about the use of water or of firecrackers. I know he has at least once built a small fire at a hole, aiming to smoke them out from under ground and put them in his ready sights. Yet still they largely have eluded him. Some days, in frustration, he consoles himself with shooting walnuts from the walnut trees. My real hope is that Young Garrett will succeed most in the cacophony he raises in making ours a place of such menace that the groundhogs will in prudence simply leave. It hasn't happened yet.

While we remain obliged to live alongside our destructive diggers, I seek what comforts I can find. I school myself in ways that groundhogs might be counted good. By now, I know all the benefits they bring, though I count these spare and inadequate to my own purposes.

Groundhogs are of course most famous for their purported predictive powers, for their emergence on Groundhog Day to let us all know what we may expect of coming weather. This seems a talent, to be sure, but not one we especially need round here – as if a farm place utterly overrun by weathermen who work one day a year could justify the destruction that they otherwise create. But groundhogs can do more than this. All that digging can be useful to the soil. Turned and aerated earth is healthier all round, preventing compacting and giving roots a chance to thrive. Still, the places ours have chosen most to dig are free of trees whose growth we would encourage, nor do the mounds of graveled earth they leave outside each hole well testify to any aid they might be offering. So rocky is our soil that they mostly turn up fresh stone to foul a mower blade.

Of the benefits that groundhogs give, the greatest by far are not for us but for others of their kind. It turns out that they are generous souls, and even as they seem to want to crowd us out, they'll play host to others who like to den up in the colder months. They let other creatures come on in, sharing their tunnels with voles and chipmunks, even foxes or, to their own detriment, coyotes. I want to find in this a good that I can prize, but wanting to think something good and really thinking it good are not the same.

The good that groundhogs give are benefits for the big of mind, for those willing and able to think of thriving in totalities. I do not want mine a land of deadened soil, nor yet would I wish mine a place where voles and chipmunks are denied warm rest in winter. I likewise understand that we, my people on this place, are but a small part of its population. Most things out here have some part to play in the elaborate overall, and it is a fool who sacrifices to human preference some bit of nature necessary to the whole. We live with traces of ill-begotten efforts to contain and manage this or that. The invasive multiflora rose against which we make ongoing war was brought in deliberately. What was thought to be good planting against erosion has now become but utter aggravation, a pretty misery that crowds out what once belonged and freely grew here. In short, small-minded mistakes already pepper the landscape for those who know its history. I do not want to be small-minded, nor to solve a problem just to make another that is worse. Yet still, I struggle. While I realize intellectually that what profits fox or vole can also profit me, I cannot make this a truth by which to live.

I started out writing all this business about our late groundhog troubles with a purpose but, as with most of my efforts, I have now drifted. Because I am supposed to be writing a book on grief and sorrow but cannot seem to write it, I inhabit the fact of this as if it is a prison. I haunt the cell of "philosophy of loss," poking round the walls and hoping for a yielding door – which is to say that I am ever on the hunt for *some way out* of mute frustration and into the writing of this thing I'm meant to write. Perhaps if one will try to write a book on loss and the sorrows that it brings, one will come to see too much in the register of those resistant struggles. This, at least, is how it is for me and for all this business with the groundhogs.

All those philosophers writing up their thoughts about death and what it means strike me as just so many fellows at the feedstore. They all have their ideas about what might make the trouble yield, and they're all probably right sometimes, but only sometimes. The best of them are sharpshooters, but even those can most days only miss. I'm sure a little Stoicism might help a bit when you want to fall apart, just as surely as smoking them out might kill a groundhog or two. But it's all just *stuff to try*, and it's all got an underlying air of foolishness about it, an atmosphere of desperation and a whiff of inept futility. If you're foolish enough to treat any one of all this stuff as a definitive solution, you can transform an ordinary trouble into disaster, burn the barn down or collapse it in a heap. Still, I thought, maybe the way into writing about grief and loss is just to own up to the fact that no one yet has worked this stuff truly out – really, that this stuff can never truly be worked out. The best you're ever going to get is a catalog of possibilities, none reliable and all in some way vexed. You can reach here to water, there to gasoline, another day to fumes. And throughout your labors and your trouble, you'll struggle still to take that wider view – the view that death, like groundhogs, has some helpful place in the overall. That elusive wider view of things won't save your ankle if you stumble in a hole, but it might console you some against the pain. It is all about the *might,* and never about what really works because nothing really does.

These were my thoughts in writing about groundhogs. See, the groundhogs were *just an analogy,* a way to frame what I could say of grief. But I won't really write of grief that way, or maybe any way at all. Each time I push against the door of this, my prison, it takes me somewhere else. Today it was to groundhogs and their several holes upon our place, of the mazes lying hidden beneath the surface of the seen. My words are like Young Garrett's shot. I pepper the page with verbal buckshot, but keep bringing back things that never were meant to be my target. I cannot kill grief, so I just harass it with my misplaced, noisy words.

18

Lay By and Store

The Lord has commanded us to lay by and store. That's what Orville Hall would always say on Sunday just ahead of passing round the collection plate at church. His words were, ever and always, just this and just the same. I was but a child then and puzzled at why God's wanting us to lay by and store should be remarked right as we were about to give up some of what we'd laid by to the church. It seemed to me that if we took this command seriously, we might want to give away less. But apart from what the words did mean, I never could decide if the tone he used was solemn and grave or just sheepish. The latter seemed more likely, as Mr. Hall was one of those men at church who seemed ill at ease with saying anything in public, his overalls unnaturally clean because it was Sunday and himself looking ready to have everyone's attention steered anywhere but toward himself. That reluctance to have all eyes on him might explain why this was the most he ever said before sending the plate around, the bare fact of the Lord's command being enough to tell us that here was the part where we would part ourselves from some of what we'd stored. As I've seen the church now pass beyond the keeping of men like Mr. Hall, I am tempted to other explanations, or at least to rue what somewhere got lost.

Mr. Hall was one of the many men of my grandfather's generation who led the church of my childhood, men who were at once quiet but also presumably in charge. They were not like the preachers or church-leader types more common today, those eager to long hold forth and hang on to people's attention, those wont to turn a prayer into a sermon as if spiritual gravity measures heaviest where more words are used. This newer type seems more motivated by want than by duty. But I'm not certain what exactly they do want. Perhaps they are but what prior generations would, in their ever-reliable economy of words, have called "stiff-necked Pharisees," ones who need not just to be upright but to perform their uprightness in sight of others. I would like to think instead that their prolonged recitations and tendency to lay down doctrine at every verbal turn bespeak anxiety about getting things right. Saying something out loud to an audience of others will tend toward firming up one's own commitments. It would indeed be nice to imagine them so awash in doubt that when they are obliged to pray out loud before others, the compulsion to piously proclaim doctrine comes on them in some too prolific desperation to want something to be true. But I can't really believe this. The new sorts don't speak doubtfully, but with conviction, and they are too often almost arrogant with it. I worry they fashion themselves as specially blessed shepherds, all too ready to corral the rest of us into truths they never do in fact doubt. I worry they're trying to save our mortal souls. I wish that they would stop. But since they won't, I just long ago stopped going to church.

Here could commence a full litany of all the reasons I quit church, and the reasons are many. They all reduce neatly, though, to not believing the things that I would be required to believe. Given all that I cannot believe, it might seem natural to find not going to church a great relief, but it has not been so. To be sure, I did in young adulthood find it a revelation of human freedom to have Sunday mornings to myself. Yoked from the cradle to the chafing harness of cleaning up, dressing up, and then sitting through it all, I initially found it a radically pleasant expansion of mortal time just to freely idle my way through Sunday mornings. I want none of the homilies now called prayer and will never find my way to shouldering the leaden doctrine that sits so heavy on the place. But I sorely do miss the confusion that did once prevail, a confusion now as decisively absent as those earnest old souls who didn't really welcome the eyes of the congregation upon them, those compelled to speak by no more than duty – someone, after all, did need to get that tin plate circulating. Since a child will naturally but dimly understand the intellectual or spiritual structures of the church even when she stands inside them, perhaps what I miss is a bafflement that only childhood itself affords.

Recollections of my childhood in church are tricky business, for memory tangles and sometimes fuses how things were then felt with how things may now feature in retrospect to one grown older. Unexamined nostalgia is one hazard, for once age has done its work and burdened one with complexity, the simplicity of a child's understanding can be mistaken for a simplicity belonging to the world itself. One thinks the world was better in some "back then," but that's only because a child's sight can't pick out the knotted convolutions and rough patches that would temper any judgments of "better." So, too, what gets offered a child in church is not what gets offered an adult. Sunday school is for stories – for parting the Red Sea with a staff, turning ladies into salt, and smiting enemies – a storehouse of phantasmagorical wonder and, I will admit, things to try at home. I never did part the creek with a stick, but the raw marvel of Sunday school stories left me utterly uninterested in attending to the prayers and sermons that followed. These were duller by degrees and largely induced a stupor only lunch would fix. Where doctrine would most flow in childhood, I had already drifted away into daydreaming about what would come next. So perhaps the gloomy tones of certain orthodoxy was ever on the place, and only when increasing age attuned my ear did I hear it. Still, the church has indubitably changed. It has indoor plumbing now.

Sometime in the 1980s the church put in a bathroom. Before this, it had but an outhouse, though one well made and better than most. Its bench seat had two holes, rather than the more typical single, one marked for boys and one for girls. I wasn't of course privy to any of the conversations that would have settled on using some of what the church had laid by to buy indoor plumbing, but I did later hear that there was considerable generational friction about whether and when to tear the outhouse down. The church's older members, those who had suffered through and outlasted the Great Depression, wanted not to waste a decent outhouse – after all, it would be useful if the indoor works broke down – while the younger members saw it as now surplus to requirements, perhaps even a bit of blight. The older sorts prevailed for a time, but only for a time, and the outhouse did eventually go the way of all things, which is to say that the spot it once occupied is now given over to more parking.

I'm not sure just where I'd place myself in the great outhouse debate. I never did like using the outhouse because no one could, nor does it seem necessary to me to store this particular bit of God's blessings. One can guard too much against the day when a thing might prove useful and an inability to discard things now replaced can work like an affliction – such can be the logic that hoarding is made of. But even as the purposive reasons for keeping the outhouse exercise little appeal, I can't help but wonder if the thing became symbolic, if readiness to part with this bit of the old church betrayed a cast of mind that had the old sorts worried. Perhaps getting rid of it just didn't make good sense to them and registered not just as imprudence but as spiritual hubris. It takes a kind of confidence to let go a resource before it is exhausted, to have done with a thing before the thing has been used up. I expect my own cast of mind is far too fanciful, but I am tempted to a theological account of plumbing. If you will let go a perfectly good outhouse, you must trust that good things endure, or at least trust that you can keep things in the shape you've made for them, a shape that includes indoor plumbing. This is reasoning about the world, about the material provisions of human existence. And it is in confidence about the world that I discern a shift from what the church once was, or at least what it once was to me.

There can come with faith an expectation that "the Lord will provide," but this belief, the philosopher in me finds, is wanting in precision. There is in it no remark on God's timing and for we finite, mortal sorts, the timing would indeed seem to matter. Accepting the claim as a comment on life as we experience it, a life beset by need and desire, means developing a high trust in the world itself or, if that really can't be on offer, in one's own ability to accept that what gets provided is still for the best. The Lord will either keep us in the funds broken plumbing needs if it will be repaired, or He will have left us with no toilet for some good reason, and any suffering induced by this we can, still and all, happily endure secure in the trust that He has provisioned us with what we really need. In either case, the broken material world essentially gets fixed – in meaning if not in fact. I suppose what stays with me most about the old church, with its taciturn and hesitant men, is that they didn't seem to have this kind of trust. Theirs was not a world to trust and they didn't seem to trust themselves in it. Things might well not work out for best or you might not be able to summon up a way to think they do.

When I was a child, church seemed more about what people did than what they believed, or more about what people *tried for* than anything they would ever claim as done. And what they most plainly seemed to try for was just to hang in there, to suffer the bewildering stuff of human life with what shared dignity they could together manage. The Sundays spent in my grandparents' tiny rural church seemed to me a time for mustering, not a marshaling of truth against uncertainty, or of faith in good when things seem bad, but of people – people who could abide a little better if they sometimes did it together. We assembled, I thought, not to solve but to share life's vexing travails, to join up in gnawing humility for a weekly collective recitation of how nothing really makes any sense. Some things that break – not just toilets, but also bodies and hearts – resist all fixing, in both fact and meaning, and this makes the world entire a place of trepidation and uncertainty. While steady, focused doctrine can lay like lead upon the soul, carrying confusion is harder still. So if you will give yourself over to confusion's weight, it's best done with others lest one be entirely bowed by it. That's what church was for. No one ever told me this was what we were doing. It was nothing announced directly or out loud, but as I try to trace my memories to their source, I find that we did sing it.

The hymns of the church were mostly sung testament to hopes simple and plain, and therefore most profound. Mostly early twentieth-century American standards, the songs confessed a longing that things may someday, somehow, just work out better than they ever seem to now. They were, I belatedly recognize, songs written in and about poverty. We'd sing of having a "home prepared," and it wouldn't be just any home but a "mansion just over the hilltop" where we'd "walk on streets that are purest gold." We'd live where "no storm clouds rise" and in a whole "city made of gold." Gold seemed to feature a lot in what we sang, and this seemed only fitting, given that the want of gold was literally posted on the church wall. At the front was hung a sign that listed not just the day's attendance and offering but the record attendance and record offering, a public pronouncement of the best the church had ever done. I don't believe the record attendance was ever above 70 or so back then, and the record offering was correspondingly small, a few hundred dollars. So our songs of mansions were sung as we faced these numbers in all their modesty, an indirect confession of how we yet neither constituted a city of any good size nor were we so flush we'd *walk* on gold. But material poverty was only the bruised symbolic skin stretched over bone-deep aches not for money but for sense – the longing to *make* some sense of why life is so often so damnably hard.

Few of the songs, at least those that stick most with me, did make sense. Instead, they ever only hoped for it – we did not sing sense but about its perennial postponement. There were lots of "somedays" and "far aways" in our songs – someday and far away marking that time hence when things might start to make sense. Meanwhile, we'd remark not just that so distant time, but the right now too, and right now was all for troubles. Our songs were all about contrasts – what we'd someday get was understood in light of what we had. To sing that "some day yonder we'd never more wander" or that "darkest night would turn to day" seemed to me a way to register hope alongside the far more fundamental admission that for now we were stumbling around lost and lightless. We'd together long to end up where "all is love," but for now we mostly only had "sad farewells" and "tear-dimmed eyes," with "all our sins and griefs to bear." One of my favorites put it all most baldly:

> Tempted and tried we're oft made to wonder
> Why it should be thus all the day long,
> While there are others living about us,
> Never molested though in the wrong.
>
> Farther along, we'll know all about it.
> Farther along, we'll understand why.
> Cheer up, my brother, live in the sunshine,
> We'll understand it all by and by.

That's a song one can whimper in some comfort, even as the hymn is all about the want of any substantial comfort.

The world it describes not only doesn't make sense, it defies sense. And its defiance is no casual or occasional resistance, no episodic opposition to what we'd prefer and want. Instead, it's just the way of things, "all day long," as the world arranges itself to favor the mean, the wrong, the people who seem always and ever to have it easier, even as they need not earn their ease. We do the best we can, we seemed to sing, we really are *trying*, but the world entire was never made to yield to this, or to us. We would thus raise a joyful noise unto the Lord, but really only to tell Him that we together have concluded that we will *not* figure this thing out. Ultimately, for me at least, the Lord was a little like that outhouse, surplus to requirements.

The songs of hope and longing that we sang always put off and postponed any resolution of substantial human confusions. They worked as exhortations to endure, to summon up the stuff to live in a world that doesn't make sense, but because we sang not as one but as a tattered, bedraggled company of the confused, they managed still to do something rather than nothing. I suppose that's why I like the raw honesty of "Farther Along" best, for even as it forthrightly says nothing makes sense, it also wants us all to cheer up about it. It's got no mansions in it, not even in the faraway, and offers instead sunshine and the companionship of the likewise confused. Notably, both of these are free. And exhorting each other to "cheer up, my brother, live in the sunshine" is, I find, both the worst and the best advice, both hard to do and the only thing one can do. Whatever confidence in the world it offers is the frailest human sort, the kind that leaves all the confusions intact but suggests there might be some good yet if we gather them together. This is why I so dislike doctrine, I suppose.

The newer church, with its stiff-necked Pharisees and their leaden doctrines, denies me my confusion. To be sure, the doctrine is all inflected toward hope. Indeed, it often features as a way to lock down hope, to make hope the thing one earns where one but thinks aright. "The Lord will provide" and you will know and trust this where your soul aligns as it should with the tedious articulations of correct belief. No more for you any irresolution about tearing down outhouses against the day when the plumbing should fail, for whatever comes of that indoor plumbing, it will have a logic doctrine can discern. The hope one here might find seems forced. Worse still, it seems to miss the most essential thing about the hardest kind of hope, the hope that has itself as target. One can hope for hope, and one hopes most for this where sense is in the shortest supply. Hope, too, is not a thing one has, but a thing one wants. That I became a "philosopher" might find explanation in all of this.

Philosophy was once a place to take confusion, though, like the church, it too is rarely like this now. The realities of contemporary academic life entail that philosophers, each by each, make incremental contributions to sorting things out, which is to say that we produce academic journal articles that seek to lock in with argumentation some conclusion we all can trust. And, because the conclusions one can most trust will, perhaps inevitably, tend toward the small and spare, our attentions turn most to truths that make a very modest difference, if they make any difference at all. To be sure, there are plenty of philosophers who would say that they do more than this, ones who earnestly believe that they make headway against confusion. Such is to say that philosophy too has its stiff-necked Pharisees, those confident that they are specially poised to dissolve confusion if the rest would only heed them. The child in me would like to smite them, or at least turn some of them to salt.

I don't know where one can now go with one's confusion and find a company really of one's kind. I long to ritualize my own confusion, to sacralize it with some others. Perhaps to sing of it and how it will abide. The need becomes more pressing as

I age because confusions do accumulate. I have so many and they do grow heavy. I have well heeded the command and they all are laid by and stored. What I need is not more of this but that part where I can part with some of them, where I can add them to the sum with others likewise toting theirs around. We could together, I am sure, make a record offering.

19

Come Home

When my grandmother Ruby died, I wanted to carry her couch to the rooftop of her house. There I would wave it about and then at last hurl it to the ground. This fantastical wish was born most basically in the mental incoherence that the fresh arrival of grief will summon, that species of confusion that can suspend all practical considerations – where, after all, would the strength to wave around a couch originate? Yet the wish was also inflected toward the aching good sense of ancient Chinese death ritual. In ancient China, when someone died, one of the bereaved would be delegated to carry her clothes to the rooftop. From that high vantage, the clothes would be waved in the air while the bereaved would ritually incant pleas for the soul of the dead to return: *Please, come back! Please, come back!* Once these pleas had failed, as fail they must, the clothes would be dropped from the roof to flutter, in the airy agony their emptiness would signal, to the ground below. The ritual was a way to act on profound longings, to make longing take a definite shape and give it over into action. And then to mark in yet more action that these, the hardest of our longings, are longings without answer.

My desire to substitute my grandmother's couch for her clothes, however impossible to achieve, was also not without its logic. For her soul might well find in this a far more provocative temptation to return. My grandmother's couch was white and thus acutely totemic, a thing that iconically remarked her in a way mere clothing never could. She had owned the couch, the *white* couch, for decades and had maintained it pristine and unblemished amidst all the dirt and grime that living on a farm entails. In the first of grief's many defeats, I thought with utter clarity: None of us still living will be equal to this couch. Best take it to the roof where her soul might see this plainly, where my deliberate abuse of it might inspire her fierce will to exercise itself back to us. *Please, come back*, but with a touch of menace better pitched to summon up an answer: *Just look what I am doing without you! You better get back here right now!*

Even in my incoherence I knew it would not work, but still it would do something like a bit of work for grief. For when her soul declined return and I cast the couch from the roof, to send it not fluttering but plummeting to earth, it would then, at long and belated last, be truly soiled, and we could thus commence in earnest with the fate now forced upon us. We would then begin the us-without-her, an us most fittingly remarked as a world in which white couches on dirty farms do not remain unblemished. As it was, the couch instead stayed firmly where it always sat, in the formal living room. Our loss was then marked carelessly rather than in ritual. Two days after her death, I noticed two long streaks of dirt across the low skirting of the couch, dirt likely come off someone's boot thoughtlessly rubbed against the cloth. The symbolism of this worked in its own shambolic way. At least it aligned well with the funeral we gave her, her plans for her own leave-taking pristine, ourselves enacting them like people clad in dirty boots.

The days that passed following my grandmother's death had been foreseen by her, at least in the broadest of their details. Ruby had planned her own funeral long before the time had come. Indeed, I think it fair to say she enjoyed the planning of it, at least a little bit. Because she died in her nineties, she had attended many funerals, and more of them at late when aging provoked thoughts of how her own might go. These many funerals, while melancholy, afforded her the opportunity to develop strong preferences where her own burying would be concerned. She had selected, well in advance, her burial clothes, her coffin, the hymns that we would sing, how the service for her should go, and the grave where we would lay her.

Ruby's burial clothing was her very best, a pale pink drop-waisted dress originally purchased for the occasion of my grandparents' fiftieth wedding anniversary party some many years earlier. It was also the dress she wore to my own wedding, a dress for which I surmise she paid a price she judged extravagant. When you have a costly best, you want to make sure you get good value out of it.

I don't now remember a single thing about that coffin and cannot divine the criteria she would have used in choosing it, though I can venture in some confidence that cost would be a factor. I like to think she chose it also for the color of its lining. My grandmother was a Spring.

Ruby was not only a farm wife, she was also a professional woman, albeit one a bit by accident. It is a commonplace among the farming people of our area to have jobs in town. My grandmother was such a one but found a success far less common with it. When her children were small, she did the sorts of side jobs many women tried. At her death, her jewelry case still contained a pin awarded her for selling Tupperware. But when her children grew less dependent, she took an entry-level job with the county social services. As anyone who knew her well might have foreseen, she was eventually running that place and, as she would, she sought to look the part – reliably turned out in fine blouses, sharp skirts and suits, her modest heels reliably matched well to her pocketbook. She dressed tasteful, not extravagant, her expenditures for her work gear mostly made at an outlet store located just over the state line in Arkansas. Looking good was important; looking good while never overpaying was a pleasure.

In the 1980s, at the height of her professional career, my grandmother's interest in dressing well took a quasi-scientific turn, which is to say she "had her colors done." There was then a fashion for having a beauty analyst take a look at you and then, in consideration of your hair and skin, telling you just what color palette should be yours. Named for the four seasons, these palette designations would then each provide a flattering map across the possibilities for human decoration. As a Spring, my grandmother had a little wheel of colored papers not unlike the cards they offer for paint samples. Across that wheel were all the colors, uniformly soft pastels, that best would suit and flatter her. For a time, it worked on her the way the Bible might – a text to be consulted in times of decision and to be revered for its sound judgments. Like all newly converted sorts, she urged both my mother and me to also have our "colors done," though as in many things, in this I also let her down and stuck with my own dogged preferences for black and grays. By the end of her life, I doubt she cared much about her colors, but still, I like to think she kept the faith, that her coffin answered to her by then archaic scripture of Spring, the satin lining selected with an eye to what would, as it so long had done, present her at her best.

The hymns that Ruby selected for her service have, like her coffin, long ago slipped from my mind. Unlike the coffin, this owes most to my own extensive mental catalog of possibilities. Mine are a people well supplied with hymns for sorrow, and Ruby's were just the ones so often sung when any of ours take leave of life. I expect we sang of flying away, or souls that never die, or leaning on Jesus, or gathering at the river, or maybe even all of these. These are hymns not just for burying, but beloved for any given Sunday. Death is but one of the woes of life, and mine are not sparing with their finest consolations. They are not just for death but for just all of it, for whatever fate or God has lately dealt us. We sang in the terrible novelty of a world without her with hymns entirely familiar, the ones no one needs a songbook to sing. Given that we are not a musical people, this was likely for the best – we would surely make bad hash of any song we'd never sung before. And in some things, it is better not to be distinct, I suppose. Ruby saved her distinct for her funeral oration, or at least tried to.

Too often in the customs of our sort, funeral orations are better just called sermons. A preacher conscripted to the task may well gesture toward the dead, to the one whose loss has put him at the podium, but he'll then at speed move on to matters much more pressing. He'll find in death a summons to warn all against a doom they may yet dodge; death is but a pretext to save the souls of we who still live. What these orations lack in acknowledgment of the newly dead, they make up for in rhetorical heat and the intensities of their setting. Hearts turned by loss toward death are then enjoined to turn away from sin and toward salvation – their own, of course, since the dead are by then either already in redemption's warm embrace or utterly beyond its reach. With all those funerals she had attended giving wind to her sails, my grandmother sailed right away from all of *that*. Her funeral oration, she was adamant, should be about *her*. And so it was, though not in a way I think she could have intended.

Ruby did not leave instructions that would identify precisely who would speak her funeral. What she left was a list of people who should *not*, a small roster of preacherly men who might well, whatever she requested, try to save us all. So it was that her nephew spoke the words to see her off. He was neither keen to do it, nor well-equipped to make the show of it that she might like. This owes not to any fault of his but to the task that he was given, one too daunting to do well. He spoke first of fearing to speak, not of the occasion itself, but of her. My grandmother was, reliably throughout her life, a power, a force before which all who once were children in her presence quailed. Such is to say that whatever his intentions, my cousin's speech functioned best to remind us all of just how terrifying Grandma was. By the time of her death, her fiercest days were long behind her, but her force and will were such to stick through time. My cousin spoke of the profound fear she could inspire, and unlike any oration that would have tried to save our souls, we could, at this and as one, do naught but agree. Her funeral thus avoided the general and commonplace stuff of fire and brimstone; the hellfire it invoked was all and only hers. In hindsight, I wish we had all called out in common chorus an emphatic Amen to that.

My grandmother was not buried in our family graveyard, this a sorrow that, like grief for her itself, holds fast. She had of course lived her entire adult life just down the dirt road from where that graveyard sits, and this, in the end, was just her problem. Since it is a rural graveyard tended only by those among the living who keep dead there, she had seen it endure years of neglect, long periods when none of the living kept it up. It would then go shabby, overgrown with grasses, fences unrepaired, the graves – as well as those within them – apparently entirely forgotten. Because of this, she buried her own parents in town, in the large and reliably maintained graveyard there. It is a place much more like the common run, regularly mown and managed, with regulations about just how the living can commemorate their dead. The most recent tombstones there have tidy inset vases in which one may leave flowers. Unlike our own graveyard, it is not a place that one may plant wildflowers or leave any idiosyncratic token of remembrance. The only flowers featuring across its sizeable landscape are false. In choosing to be buried there, she well knew all of this, for she annually purchased false bouquets to place upon her parents' rest. When I was a young child, I remember going with her and remember, too, puzzling why her parents, my Mimi and Papa, were buried so far away – when you are young, the half-hour drive to town will feel like hours. In age, I have a better sense of time and distance, yet still I rue the miles between us and that place. The distance seems not physical but metaphysical. My grandmother is buried where we can only be but visitors, people come into town from country, our offerings restricted to the tidy and the tamed.

My grandmother wanted to be buried where someone would keep her grave, where the risk of untended wilds would not threaten to consume her. This wish is at once perfectly in keeping with her life and temperament, but also remarks a difference between her and all of us. She is buried in a white couch. I wish that I could say in confidence that in choosing so she underestimated us, that we would never leave her grave neglected, diminished into overgrowth and at risk of disappearance. But time is long and we none of us can offer what a graveyard kept by salaried strangers would. If she had stayed among us, we would have made her grave a riot of real color, of flowers that not only bloom but also fade. But for how long? We will not last the way that graveyard in the town will do. And however much she organized her own leaving of this life, she could not organize us entire, not for how long death will last. I do not think her plans have worked in a way that she could wish. We are not in that sterile graveyard as we are in ours. We visit too rarely and too quickly. Unlike our own, it is not a place fit for an idle. We replace false flowers when they fade, and then return back to the wilds where we, as she once did, spend out our lives. I wish that I could call her back to us.

20

The Supply Closet of Glory

One of the first funerals I attended as an adult was for a friend. I was then in my early twenties, as was he, and we were both in graduate school. He was studying in an MFA program to become a writer, though like most who do such things, a writer was already what he long had been. But in his program, he was training with others more experienced in the art, published poets and novelists. These would come to serve as his pallbearers.

There is much from that funeral that has stayed with me in the way that nightmarish experiences tend to stick around like haunting specters. But the poet pallbearers seemed symbolic of the experience entire, men of words transformed by the ritual into mere silent muscle, the carriers of a coffin with a fellow of their kind inside and, also, silent. There were of course words spoken at the funeral, but whatever artfulness was found in them was mostly accidental and inadvertently awful. A Baptist preacher delivered an oration meant to comfort and to save our souls, but one designed on bland theology and absent any sign or signal that here was not just death, but a death most particular and terrible. As the preacher crested on the wave of hope his own belief would promise, he bellowed a line that

I have long struggled to forget: *The supply closet of glory is never empty!* For emphasis and in case we missed his shout, he repeated it in a hissing stage whisper: *The supply closet of glory is never empty!*

I have never known just how to think of this, nor did I then. At the time, the line lodged in me like a riddle I could not hope to solve. In truth, it still seems so. I have carried it with me now for decades. At best, I can think it the ugly step-cousin of Yeats' encomium on the Irish rebellion in 1916, his claim that "a terrible beauty is born." *Terrible beauty* is a phenomenon recognizable, at least to me, particularly in mourning. A supply closet stocked with, of all things, *glory* might work the same? Like Yeats, perhaps that preacher intended his arresting juxtaposition – in the preacher's case, a sublime achieved where the holy or sacred is located in the banal and comparably profane, the glory he invoked not somewhere hard and out of reach, but just there, alongside the brooms and mops. Or, perhaps the preacher's association of these unlike things was more directly and straightforwardly revelatory. We go to the supply closet when we need to replenish what is gone or to clean a mess that we have made. That day we buried my friend was without glory and plentiful with mess. The preacher intimated that there could be a way to *fix* that, a restoration *right there*, somehow. But in life I've not found that closet or anything like. I've mostly felt that funeral oration to be a small tragedy carelessly set atop a far greater. That speech was all the evidence that anyone could need to know my friend was well and truly dead – the poets all gone mute and in their silence naught but cheap "salvation," glory turned to tedium.

The early Confucians were, if anyone can be counted so, adepts at seeing off the dead. They thought that mourning just might be the signal challenge of a life. Loss will change you, so best to manage the chaos that can follow, best to codify in careful ritual the seismic alterations a life will undergo when death has taken some of it apart. My academic study of them set me to thinking of just what, if anything, could count as a *good* funeral. Like them, I do think making our grief communal and shared is vital, that it somehow matters in sorrow that we not shoulder it each alone. But beyond this rather anodyne and abstract idea resides the disruptive and all too definite reality of actual people.

Death ritual is, as they say, "for the living." Yet we the living are rarely, if ever, of the same mind. Where one finds comfort, another may find the agonies of absence. Where some find succor, others find utter loneliness made yet worse. "The living" are a desperate, disagreeing lot – and this does not change when time comes to gather round their common dead. Worse still, the singular absence of our dead is turned into a plurality. As we gather and inevitably speak of the dead, what we make of them is rarely in good alignment. Some find comfort in making the best of the dead, denuding them of their vexing complexity so that sorrow can be cleaner. Some find only aggravation in the cleaned-up dead, in the altogether too tidy summations of a life and character. The lost mother is, for one, sentimentally reduced to a tender baker of cookies, while another rues the loss of just the fractious temper served up alongside the chocolate chips. The lost friend is, for one, a person who "was always there for me"; for another, friendship rested on vigorous, agonistic exchanges and enlivening discomfort. Ritual obliges us to speak together of one who was never one alike to each and all of us. No person is their whole person with everyone; each is a mosaic. We bury the whole person, but speak in fragments – too often in fragments tamed. We lose an originality but too often verbally bury a type. Such is to say that while I am intellectually convinced that shared death ritual is a good, I mostly find in it irritation and alienation. I am coming to think that perhaps this is its point and purpose.

Once loss comes along and wrecks the world we find familiar, it might be useful if some scraps of the old stay steady and remind us that not all is lost. Wherever people gather, they chafe against each other in their differences of need and of desire. This might be a thing to count on as reliable in an unreliable world. This may be even true, or even especially true, where they are bound by love for one they hold in common and have in common lost. What comforts one may roil another; where one finds hope, another finds but despair. Unalike in life, we do not become so in our losses, though our abiding differences can at least recall to us that not all is changed or lost. Death ritual may be a way to seek the steady in a world gone on the tilt, and maybe the exact nature of the steady does not have to matter much. Maybe a world steady in its irritations counts for something. This, at least, is what I'd like to think. The supply closet of human irritations, perhaps, really is never empty.

21

Nod Line

Out in the country, the standards for what counts as a crowd or for solitude are just different. The distances between home-places mean that people a couple of miles off might qualify as neighbors: When there aren't that many people about, you roll up more, from more distant quarters, to count as people related to you by neighborly association. This is one way of making necessity a virtue. Since the general isolation of living in the country means you don't have people strictly nearby on whom to rely when need strikes, you just widen out what counts as "nearby" and thereby expand the range of people who can depend on each other. Despite having plenty of neighbors, the distances between them inevitably make for certain styles of isolation and, correspondingly, certain styles of registering that isolation.

When my husband was first coming to the farm, he initially believed we knew everyone we passed on the rural highway. For they all waved at us in passing and we all waved back, the "wave" itself a characteristic Ozark raising of your index finger off the steering wheel to give a modest, low-effort salute. At first, Garret would ask, "Who's that?" But when he often enough heard "I don't know" in response, he realized that waving at other drivers – whoever they might be – is just the done thing. This is what sociologists characterizing low-population areas call living below the "nod line": "Any community below the line, and hence below a certain size," Erving Goffman explains, "will subject its adults, whether acquainted or not, to mutual greetings; any community above the line will free all pairs of unacquainted persons from this obligation." The language here is regrettable, as I don't think any feel particularly *subjected* to the practice of waving, with all the chafing and confinement that implies, but the broader idea is surely right. If you don't see people very often, when you do see some, you tend to acknowledge them. But of course some of the ways isolation gets registered do confess a bit of chafing.

Becoming accustomed to seeing very few people does some work on perception and measurement, and it won't take very many people to constitute a veritable hoard. I knew this even as a child. When a couple of people had stopped by the house over the course of a day, my grandmother would irritably protest, "It's been just like Grand Central Station in here!" We don't get much traffic to the house or even the roads, so it won't take much to seem like a lot. Driving along the rural highway last week, my uncle and I had to completely stop the car to await our chance for a left-hand turn, a claustrophobic pause so rare that it led him to uneasily remark, "New York City must be empty today. They're all out here on this road."

The typical solitude and scarce population of the country can render you unready for even the sparest indications that other people exist. Forced to encounter them, one feels pinched, hemmed in, as if one were in an urban metropolis obliged to bump up against total strangers in a rat maze of crowded humanity. Invocations of New York City might be a touch hyperbolic when you can still count the people you encounter on one hand, but they do capture an occasional sense of being overwhelmed. All human beings are creatures of induction, working our expectations to fit what we most usually find and experience, so the disruption of even a few people when one is used to none is still a disruption. In some ways, the country can feel more hemmed in than a city.

Many years ago, my brother regaled me with an oddball story he'd read about a man on a quixotic crusade against television. This man believed that the television was working untold horrible effects upon us all because it was full of little people. He wasn't so far gone that he believed the little people on a TV screen are *real* people, but he did believe that having small moving images of people so often in your sightline was going to disable the good exercise of our animal abilities to be alert to actual-and-present other people. Evolution, he surmised, had worked in us a strong and prudent instinct to take note of other human beings in our visual space. And TV was messing all that up – the unrelenting ubiquity of tiny, fake screen people would dull our capacity to notice big, real, present people and whatever threats or opportunities they might portend. Out in the country, I think of that man awash with anxiety about our collective, decaying animal abilities. I think he would find in us some succor. For we still see and notice all it seems – even the tiniest of people, which is to say each other spied from across even substantial distances.

Our pastures sit where they are easily sighted from the dirt road, so it's not uncommon to have neighbors remark on what they've seen us doing, even as our own experience is of working out in a field all alone. Garret and I have been praised as hard-working by people we only see to speak to maybe once every few weeks. They pass by our place, see us out working, and draw conclusions based on observations we don't even know they're making. The sense of being unwittingly observed by others is of course unsettling in a context where it is sometimes necessary to pee outdoors – one then wants not to be an accidental TV star for one's neighbors – and this marks a significant difference between our figurative versions of Grand Central Station and that real place in New York City. In New York, anything you're doing – really, probably almost anything – will likely be swamped by the superabundant waves of humanity, obscured from anyone's notice because it's happening in a sea of other human stimuli. Not so in the country. We are isolated, but that's a far cry from hidden. Hidden profits from crowds, and we lack those.

Even as other people can feature with an outsized prominence in what might superficially seem an isolated life, what I most notice is how many different ways there are to be alone. There's a yarn that used to circulate about an Indigenous Alaskan language that had multiple different words to describe that stuff we collect into the single word "snow." I don't know whether that is an accurate rendering of any Indigenous Alaskan language, but this example used to be trotted out as a way to remark that where people live in close contact with a phenomenon, they tend to parse it far more finely, to divide it up and treat as many a thing that others might just see as one. If you live with snow a lot, you'll come to have different ways to express how many different styles of snow there really are; close and prolonged experience will awaken you to variety, and you will want language to catch at all that variety. We don't get enough snow to need more than the usual word for it, but I have come to think our farm needs a richer vocabulary for all those ways of being that presently pass as just "alone."

My lexicon of aloneness would, I think, need to capture both the practical and existential, the usual and the surprising. I would first need words for all the ways there are to be alone in work. There is of course the rather empty sort of solitude that comes with working well to do some chore. When the work goes smoothly and is agreeably hard enough, solitude becomes a pleasing sort of nothing, for the lines between oneself and what one does blur and dissipate. To lose oneself in work can work a transformation of a sort, as if to be alone like this is not to be at all. There is naught but process, and whatever one would call one's "self" recedes or gets forgotten. This is a rather

Buddhist sort of solitude and maybe if I had it often enough, I'd come to think like them and decide I have no self at all. But my more usual styles of being alone in work do not tickle at the edges of enlightenment. They instead scratch and claw against my limitations.

I need a word for what it's like to be alone in work beyond one's ken and capabilities. Or maybe I need many words for this, as my deficits are many and diverse. Sometimes solitude is made acute by want of strength, as when one is alone with work that two could do but one cannot. The farm is well supplied with things that need to be shifted, lifted, or carried, and there is a grunting style of aloneness, felt in the abdomen and back, when one tests one's solitary self against the big or heavy but to fail and fail again. It is a frustration felt both with oneself and by oneself to recognize that what one seeks to do cannot be done alone. This is a bodily aloneness, but there are mental forms of this as well. Some intellectual problems resist all shifting when one must shift alone. In my experience, these are mostly mechanical. Alone with a tractor that will not start, one can ask the heavens why, but I have yet to find an answer in this way. That old Greek Socrates was wont to say that wisdom comes with knowing what you do not know. But wisdom of this sort does not start tractors, and so to be alone with it, finely aware of all one does not understand, is not a triumph but travail. The self that one finds in solitudes like these, alone with work one cannot do, is a tangle of frustration, and to be alone this way is hard to bear. This in part explains another way to be alone in work: when left alone with limitations, one passes into active peril.

Faced with work one cannot do alone straightforwardly, one can always go for help, and this I sometimes do. Indeed, upon reflection I think a word is needed here as well, a term to capture resignation's sweet relief. Having accepted that I cannot budge the truck where it sits stuck in the muddy bottoms, the long walk to fetch the tractor to drag it out is a solitary walk

I tend to like. Giving up resistance to the inevitable yields a special quieting of the mind. This is the solitude of respite, that open, empty space between what one could not solve and the coming of solution. Giving up when giving up is right is to shuffle off a burden, to pass unscathed through perils that otherwise might come. (There are dumber ways to try to free the truck than walking for the tractor.) I wish I had the wisdom to release resistance when I ought. But instead frustration with my limitations too often has me doing what I shouldn't, keeping up the fight where not just wisdom but even dull prudence would surrender.

It is a blunt and unforgiving fact that when one works in isolation, one will sometimes need to be creative. Where help is distant or unavailable, one sometimes just makes do, but making do can also mean doing what is foolish. There needs to be a term for aloneness turned to menace or to folly that could prove fatal. This would be the word I'd hurl as I slide toward the edge of the barn roof, knowing that if I fall there will be none to hear. It would be the word I whisper underneath the brushhog as I tug tangled barbed wire from its blades and hope belatedly that the hydraulics don't fail me now. It would be the word I sigh on reading in the local paper of an elderly man who died while burning brush. Just as I have often done, he stumbled and fell. Alone and tired with a fire, the direction that one falls makes all the difference – fall away and one can stumble finally home when work is done, fall in and you are done. Perhaps that needs a word all of its own as well. There is a difference that makes all the difference between the solitude that merely menaces and the kind that kills. There, too, the kind that kills might itself need some more exact parsing.

Accidental death in work undertaken on one's own might need to be distinguished from other ways to die alone. A sudden stroke or heart attack will of course be fatal where none are by to hear and help. And one can't count out the deaths that still could come when you think you are alone but aren't. I think of this latter sort when I flush an animal while at work. So far I've only startled deer, rabbits, armadillos, and at worst skunks, but there are bears about. I hope to never startle one of those. I once sat passing time by reading while I waited for a fire I'd set to calm and die. Adrift in some written world and inattentive to my own, I gazed up from the page at last to find a coyote standing near. He stared at me and I at him for longer than I liked. His ambling off at last was like a gift, though I did not again that night feel quite alone. So there needs to be a word for that, for what it's like to be alone with creatures not one's sort. That word would have an eerie cast, as would the word for the strange solitude that comes in some collapse of time.

When I am all alone at work, I sometimes almost see myself. Traversing that field where we'd play spies, some unsettling transformation takes the place, and I can see and hear her there. Her legs are flayed with scratches from running in the hay, her hair is flat with sweat, and the freckles have come out in summer force. She's all alarm and hissing "*Brezhnev! Brezhnev!*" – she is a child of the Cold War, and if you will heroically spy on your enemies, he would be the one to watch. Or she's sitting just there outside the barn, idly scratching at her arm while I work, her lap a pile of cats. She always was one for trying to tame the barn kittens, and she probably has ringworm on that arm. I've found her laying in a feed bunk, with her arms crossed against her chest and a solemn expression on her face. She's pretending to be dead again, but she will not close her eyes. Death, she thinks, works best if your coffin is open to the sky and you can watch the clouds pass by. Sometimes she's up that tree alongside the farmhouse, sometimes she's by the creek idly throwing stones. Sometimes I imagine she's gotten out of the truck just as I have gotten in.

Farm trucks have a distinctive smell that I can only struggle to describe. Some of the elements involved are plain to say: the odors are of earth, of grass, of sweat sunk into tattered seats to dry. But these also mix and mingle with the smell of metal warmed in sun and with a whiff of gas or grease. The combination is distinctive but quickly lost. I only smell it when the truck has set long closed up in heat and it quickly dissipates as soon as the windows are rolled down. It smells like my grandfather. It smells of 1978 or maybe '79, and some trip we took to town to the feedstore, me on the bench seat beside him, back when driving was to me a mystery made more elaborate by the tall stick he shifted with brown hands. Alone inside my truck and with that smell, I'm neither here nor way back there, but in that collapse of time that has me in the company of my ghosts and yet so terribly alone. This is an elusive and uncertain form of solitude, and it is too much everywhere found upon the farm. I have it like a second sight that really doesn't work, as if there are many of my own about, residing just beyond the edges of my vision. They are that thing one almost spied but quickly lost, that thing you think you see but only if you do not truly look: My grandmother with her back to me, her attention on the stove, the shoulder straps and tie of her faded apron limp, a flick of spoon into the lard pot that also, now, isn't really there. My uncle, squint-eyed from the smoke curling from his cigarette, pacing out the steps to the shop, not wanting a word but only the nod that characterized his favorite style of greeting. My grandfather in his cap and also in an apron, his of some salvaged rubber stuff he's knotted into place with a bit of twine, and another smell, the dusty milky scent of calf formula, himself at the barn sink, sliding orange nipples onto warm bottles big as bread loaves.

If you see someone in just some place enough, the place may come to feature something like them, even when the place outlasts them. There needs to be a word for this. The word I want would have to make a hash of whatever boundary rests between utter, aching loneliness and the harassments of a crowd, between the living and the dead. It would be a word that sometimes would protest, "The graveyard must be empty today for all my ghosts are up here on this farm." But it would also be a word to carry some lament, some call that finds no answer, some clumsy reaching into empty air – a word of passing. It would be a word you lose just as you try to say it.

My ghosts only exist because I do, because I saw them here and see them still, their shades and traces on the place. I assume it was the same for them - that with them perished all of those they saw when there was none to see. I never see my great-grandparents – Will in the shop with baseball on the radio while he pretends to do some work, or Della in the garden with a bucket full of peas that she'll carry to the shade to shell. I like to think my grandfather did see that, saw them, those whom I can only count as the ghosts of my own ghosts. Working on the place as they had done, maybe he sometimes spied them lasting out beyond their lives in work that passed from them to him. But when he died, so, also, would those shades and all their traces. The dead, too, are mortal creatures, and there's another grief in this. My ghosts can't last because I won't.

Thoughts like these leave me with myself again – not young and scratched and chasing communists but old as I am now. I am not the seer of myself, but still and all, I come now to glance at something of myself just out of sight, myself made but a trace and then become a trace that's lost. No word for that, nor need of it.

22

Some Sort of Deal

Some of my impulse to write philosophy that includes the stuff of life as I now lead it – to write of my homeplace, farm, and family – is just the way the world at large gets people like them wrong. A friend of mine, experienced in publishing, once told me that "no one wants to read about poor rural whites struggling to walk upright." Hers was a bitter commentary on an age all out of sympathy, a time of politics gone sour. But her claim, I have since found, is not exactly right. People do wish to read of the benighted white and rural poor, but what they read must have a certain cast of mind. The flavor is of quasi anthropology, sometimes with a dash of pity, but more often horrified and just a bit agog. The caricature is often all. Ubiquitous journalistic visits to the diner tell us of the talk that happens over coffee, the diner not unlike a zoo where one might observe the wild and the dangerous in a setting controlled for one's own safety. Here is the 70-year-old farmer in stained Wranglers and worn boots. He speaks now of immigration, now of the terrible elites, now of conspiracy, and all in utter ignorance. His peer in bibs and camouflage hat will nod along and complain of Washington, of taxes, and those feminists. It isn't that the zoo reports are wrong, but that they are all of a piece, and that piece is such a fragment. I know the sorts who congregate with coffee, some to resent the world beyond their ken and kind. But I have no tidy explanation for them, nor wish to turn my meager understandings in a direction that might try. Yet since the world that I would write is a world that does and must include them, they work a kind of poison in me as I consider what it means to write.

Writing is rarely something singular or definitive. One tries to say what one would say, but if one has a reader, the reader will and must interpret. She must make of what one says what she can or will. To write as I would do, about the Ozarks and my people there, is to invite misunderstanding. Whether come from me in the writing or from the reader in the reading, a caricatured morality presently seems to stalk us all.

One of our friends out in the country has a turn of phrase that I have come to like. He appends "sort of deal" to all manner of expression and idea. Sometimes for clarity, he adds, the question-not-a-question, "if you know what I mean?" Lately, as we talked about the southern pasture closest to the creek, he said the new fencing needed would be "a winter sort of deal" – a thing to do when other work is idled by the season and the cold. Of his son's recent success he mentioned it was more of a talent than a hard work sort of deal. Our need to address some invasive species troubling another pasture were a time-and-cost sort of deal. With him, there are few things that need genuinely to be specific. It is good and serviceable enough to locate what *sort of deal* we must contend with. The phrase is gestural, at once taxonomic and in defiance of any exacting taxonomies we would assign the world or ourselves. (I have come to want philosophy to address, mostly if not entirely, things that are some sort of deal, and this is why I lately cannot do philosophy at all.) Very little, I find, situates cleanly or well in the tidy categories we might make. Perhaps more pointedly, I dislike the effort and impulse to place things so, to make them answerable to our easiest maps of understanding. But should I say too much more of our friend and his looser and therefore better epistemic practices, all I write here will become prey to the rapacious new morality, a beast devouring all – at least the "all" that presently comprises the things of which I would aspire to write.

One is allowed the nonjudgmental eye only if one will report and at least pose as seeking understanding. But I have here confessed to friendship with just the sort "we" should dislike – my friend could opine in a diner if he only had the time. I am even being cagey in my description of him just to save him, and myself. Say too much about his views and I will damn us both, him for what he thinks and me for liking him anyway. I am too proud for that result, or even for its risk. In truth, I am a moral philosopher utterly exhausted by the moral, by its intrusion into every corner of our lives. That's not exactly right. I have long thought that the moral is more pervasive than any of us in our right minds should like. But therein lies the rub for me.

A couple of years ago, when we were leaving our home in town to travel to our farm, we left our garbage cans at the curb for collection day. Since we would not be home to put them back along the house, we asked a neighbor, another academic, if she would do it for us. Then ensued the hedging, great reluctance we have now come to expect – she could do it, she supposed in a tone altogether too beset, her voice and face communicating that she would try heroically to suffer this inconvenient imposition. We would owe her for this. It would tax her.

Around that same time, my father's workhorse came up with a flat, a dire situation for one who can so barely, and only in great pain, walk. Our country neighbor spied the flattened tire and had it off and thrown in the back of the truck to take to town to patch before my father even knew of it. Our neighbor has both a town job and a never-ceasing burden of farmwork, but when he saw that flat, he judged it a necessity sort of deal, so he just took care of it.

Even as I make these lines across the page, my inner critic hisses the objections. My imagined readers all appear as cynics – worse, as moral predators, their muscles tensing for the lunge and pounce. Fixing a lame old man's tire might be nice, but it cannot redeem the moral rot of being a redneck conservative; who cares about your trash cans if your neighbor votes the way she ought?

So much of what presently passes for intellectual and cultural discourse would have us all as beasts. Or perhaps we all are gods. But gods of the kind that I was reared to fear: beings both confident and decisive in their judgment, ready to hurl away the wrong as damned. My most reliable friends are mostly just those damned. My less reliable friends might well condemn me if they knew. Writing is an exposure, and I so often feel too exposed to the casual, cavalier and purist judgments of others to begin it. This is why I also cannot join Twitter or whatever it's called, or what things have lately come to take its place. I did join Facebook and there see far too much of how my educated peers treat and talk of those who would speak sometimes warmly of the damned. To the purist, I am one who not only dwells in but enjoys bad company. It isn't that I morally approve of my friend's worst ideas, it's that his worst ideas aren't all he is. Human beings are an altogether vexing sort of deal and I distrust our tendencies to simplify them onto sides.

Moral ills are both great and small, and all over in between. So, too, our moral goods. My own efforts to suss out what boundaries we should keep and what boundaries we should cross have collapsed in weariness. I am not principled with it, but I want not to shun a neighbor. And I don't especially want to explain that, much less offer up some justification. Before I even can begin, I am too weary. Writing feels like a trap, but one that I can see, so why step in it? It has become a save-yourself-the-grief sort of deal, if you know what I mean.

23

Best Keep It

I have long been vexed by some of my inheritance and, most specifically, at the vast collection of wheels my grandfather left behind. I sometimes wonder if I could profit from a prolonged study of those wheels once his, now mine. I have an abundance and stand ready, should need arise, to make all manner of things roll instead of scoot or drag. I have wagon wheels, chair wheels, toy wheels, wheels of metal, wood, and plastic, wheels with rubber cushioning and wheels without. If I just stared at them long enough, I might at last discern in them something more than the ordinary I could do, some way to turn them toward uncommon account and make them perform feats unpredictable but useful. This, after all, explains why Grandpa accumulated and kept them. He was never one to discard anything that "still has use in it." If this was a scholarly paper, I'd need to put a footnote here and clarify that "use" must be understood in a nonstandard way and to ambitiously encompass all styles of utility presently in operation and, also, all styles of utility not yet but maybe later to be discovered. My grandfather was a magpie. His theory of utility amounted to: You never can tell, so best keep it. This explains why we have for years had a Barbie doll head on a nail outside the barn office. Barbie is there, patiently awaiting the day that someone around here discovers a good and fruitful use for her head.

My impulse to study all those wheels once his, now mine, issued from a melancholy longing. Perhaps a focused spell of contemplation that took them as my target would transform me. Like Saul on the road to Damascus, I might find revelation and discern at last just what those wheels are for. They would "call to me" and then I could commence with some surely miraculous feat of ingenuity of the sort my grandfather habitually pulled off. I would create . . . something, I don't know what, but it would be something needing lots of wheels. Once done, I could move on to my even vaster store of hinges.

My grandfather Lynn had a gift, much exercised upon the farm entire, for making much of little and making do with whatever was to hand. He would not buy what he could make and he would not hire what he could do. But if one will live this way, one must get clever at making and doing, and this is what he was. He was a natural practitioner of what military sorts call "field expediency" and what the psychologists would call "divergent creativity," two artful sounding expressions for using whatever one can find to hand in ingenious, nonstandard ways.

My grandfather built the farmhouse himself, a fact that is told all over its arrangements. It is full of things not bought but found. The windows and floors were salvaged from an old hotel gone to ruin. The chimneys are built of native stone, collected from our farm's abundance of that stuff. The finest walls are made of golden oak harvested from our woods. These are visually pleasing bits, but the hidden spaces confess a creativity of another order.

When the farmhouse doorframes were removed to replace them with new, we found an explanation for the chill the doors permitted, for my grandfather had insulated the doorframes with his old clothes. Work denims were stuffed into the walls in dusty testament to his desire to keep out the cold but not spend a penny doing it. Likewise, my grandfather did not let the fact that he was no trained electrician stop him from wiring his own house and barns. None of the electrical outlets were grounded, but he solved this by shearing off that third prong on every device he owned that had one. A professional electrician called in after my grandfather died to address a problem demurred when asked if the place was safe as is. "Only if it's understood that I was never here and we never spoke of this," he said. A similar caution all my own forbids my trying out my grandfather's table saw. He constructed it out of a washtub, mower engine, truck leaf springs, and old barn oak. Other tools he built we keep still in use.

The post-hole digger – better than any bought version we've ever tried – is welded out of heavy metal poles and bits he presumably had laying around. Like others of the tools he made – mostly shovels, pickaxes, and hoes – its outrageous weight turned out to be an asset. Some of his tools have not endured – the candy-cane striping on tools he made from scavenged swing-set poles lent work a certain jaunty dash but lacked the sturdiness to last. Others still are hard to use and testify to the fact that he also found them so – say, when he inserted discarded calf bottle nipples into pole tops to soften up rough cuts he made in welding. Some of his creations were made for pleasure rather than for work. He constructed a homemade camper trailer, a wooden box that opened into a two-bed tented little house, the tent complete with a screen of garish purple peridot fabric he bought on sale and sewed himself. I still have his winter sled, a heavy thing that gets its speed from chisel plow blades adapted to the purpose. He crashed that sled through ice on one of the ponds when he took us grandchildren out to try it and had to walk home with pants going stiff from pond water freezing as he walked.

Had Grandpa's life been different, had he made it away from the farm for more than war service, he might have been an engineer. He once confessed to me that he wished he'd had more schooling. His education was typical for the time and area, but there were signs he could have used some more. One year, he was released from school some eight weeks early because, the teacher said, he had already learned all that his grade would have to offer and might as well not come. He would certainly have a made a good engineer, though I can't help but think that had he been formally trained, he might have lost the mental spark that had him organizing a world of bits and pieces cobbled together in ways no formal engineer could tolerate. An engineer could have produced that wiring or that saw, but simply wouldn't, training truncating daring.

My grandfather's mind laid swerves where others follow well-trod paths. The world he left behind is not just stocked with all his swerves but with abundant stuffs for more. In my less capable hands, the stuffs have indeed been made over into new, but not a new that I can like. They are hard material gone soft, useful things made totemic of a loss and so no use at all. They are no longer stuff, but symbol. Those wheels reproach me for this ineffective, wasteful transformation.

My grandfather was an intoxicating sort of person. We children, and the farm dogs too, would stalk and follow him, a mute magnetic pull drawing us along. I can't speak for the dogs, but for myself I wanted just to see what would come next, and to occupy the mostly total silence in which whatever came would happen. He was garrulous with things, but not ever with his words. And this comes to feel like explanation for the gap between us, him and me.

I think I made some mistake along the way, inheriting my grandfather's accumulating nature but directing it to words, not things. I have magpied up a storehouse of language, a place stuffed with the oddments of memory and offcuts of philosophy, a noisy mess now furring over with a melancholy dust. Even as it seems like a mistake, I can't bring myself to throw it out as useless. You never can tell, so best keep it. Or write it.

Stuff the walls of time with worn-out learning; keep out something of the chill, even if you can't entirely defeat it. But where among these words can I find a calf bottle nipple to soften up the grip? Where the means to shear off the third prong of fruitless thinking?

24

Comrades That So Long Have Gone

Working as a philosophy professor inevitably means brushing up against Greatness. I'm not entirely sure I believe in Greatness, much less its far more exalted cousin, Genius, but if you will do philosophy, you won't escape those select human beings whose words and work long outlast their lives. Aristotle's old bones turned to dust millennia ago, yet still we puzzle over all he said. When I was younger and first learning, I found it magical the way that made things and storied lives will last. What must it be like, I'd think, to write a book someone will read some thousands years hence? Did those who did such things know or have any indication? As I have aged, I've come to see it all more complicated.

Human beings are frail and fragile things, yet some will work on us like near immortals. They do what others can't or won't, and we pay them back with memory. They so impress us that we keep them, finding what they did of such account we'll spend some portion of our own finite mortal hours puzzling it out. One way to think of this is to find it all a curse of sorts. Some would say the trouble with long-dead Greatness is just the way it preys upon a living mind, establishing a yearning to do something we could hope will last. We none of us can live forever, but one might flee or fight the sorry fact by reaching to be remembered. A philosopher might explain much about the vagaries of human conduct in just this way, seeing in our most ambitious doings a plea against forgetting, a strategy to last beyond ourselves. That might be right, but I find it unappealing and too simple. The Greats stick around because we stick with them, keeping alive their doings for ourselves. And we keep most alive just the bits of them we like.

Part of what I notice now I'm older is how choosy memory can be. The nigh immortal Greats with whom I pass my working hours are so much cleaner than the living. We run them through a filter of forgiveness, we scrub them down and save what's best, preserving most what does them credit. So even as we talk of Aristotle still, we largely overlook his worst ideas – ignoring, say, his insistence that women are as irrational as children. When obliged to register such flaws, we can maybe find in them some consolation. Even the Great, we can assure ourselves, had their limitations. Old Aristotle himself can be of aid in understanding this. Even the very good, he did observe, will have *akrasia*, an occasional inability to let reason rule the day, for they too suffer their own weaknesses of will. However great the Great, they would sometimes be "incontinent," the English term used for the Greek *akrasia* (and a word I expect gives Aristotle's translators a soothing scatological laugh). None escape; the Great too will suffer incontinence. So it was for Aristotle and so it was for my great-uncle Imon.

One night some years ago as I set in hospital with my grandfather in one of his last illnesses, we talked of travel he had undertaken. Grandpa was reflecting on the present ease of travel compared to what it once had been, back when the lack of roadside services could make all manner of inconvenience. In aid of the comparison, he described a trip he took with Imon. Their course one day of driving was fractured and fragmented by the repeated need for urgent stops, for Imon had "underestimated his prune intake and come up with the trots." There was more he told than this, but his scandalizing recitation of all the facts I do not need to detail here. The finer content of the story matters not, what matters is the fact of it.

My great-uncle Imon, my grandmother's brother, was an educated man. He spent his life fulfilling ambitions far beyond the class to which he was born. He was a professor of English at a little college and there taught generations of Iowa youth the arts of composition. In my childhood, I found him a man of great remove from all the rest, a family anomaly in both his learning and his manner. I suspect he would have found this right and fitting. His parents prized him as a triumph and I expect he thought it apt they did. He was, in short, a pompous-seeming man, but one who had indeed done more than his origins would predict. He was just the sort who might, in a family such as mine, become a Great, one whose doings stand as credit to himself and perhaps to all of us. But as my grandpa spoke, I understood that it would not be so. Imon's interest for we the living would just then, and likely always, be his trots. This owes not to any meanness or desire to draw low the high. Instead, it speaks the choosiness of memory and how for us that choosing tends. In my family, historical memory about our ancestral dead has a rather definite direction. It largely does not matter what you do, however bright or noble your achievements, we'll find the bit we want and what we want will be what is peculiar. This has proved to be quite useful for us all.

To lodge oneself among broad culture's Greats, to imagine that lineage as one's own, will be chafing and unpleasant. Far happier to be joined where what gets saved is what's peculiar because "peculiar" anyone can surely do. I expect it may be hard to fall afoul of such a standard for remembrance. To be sure, not all excel – Imon's trots are modest stuff where family memory is concerned, and many others well outdid him. But there may in fact be no way to fail along our standard, for should you fail to be sometimes odd, you would be truly odd indeed. I don't aspire to Imon's "deeds" of course, no more the others', but I find great comfort in the style of our remembering. Our filters for our dead leave them all their troubles and even their indignities, so they better serve as succor for the living. I at least have found it so and found it most among our women.

My great-grandmother Della died long before I was born, so all I know of her is what my family would tell. They've told some other scattered bits and pieces, but what gets told the most is just her temper. Della once chased her husband Will across the house wielding a carving knife. She also violently thrashed a neighbor in her garden, just ran that woman to ground among the peas and tomatoes and, apparently, kicked her ass. This is what I know of Della, what family memory has collectively elected to preserve. The why of these events is always left out in the telling – no one living knows what might have provoked her, what it was that summoned up her fists and knife. I heard these stories once related as evidence that Della took the hormonal changes of aging hard. But more usually, since it all came out all right, no time is spared thinking about what Della's temper might portend, as if women after their husbands with knives is just one of those things that can sometimes happen, and happen really to anyone.

Another great-grandmother, Dovie, had troubles never quite specified. It is generally acknowledged within the family that something was awry with her nerves. Having something awry with our nerves is likely a collective family trait, a tempting explanation for why we prefer to sit with our backs to walls and cannot abide a WalMart. Yet Dovie's nerves were a different order of magnitude.

Dovie was, in the general way of most, a moral woman, but she feared being bad and feared committing The Mortal Sin most of all. The greater trouble was that she professed not to know what The Mortal Sin could be. It was, to Dovie's way of thinking, something you might just stumble into the way you might a gopher hole, a thing you'd know you'd done only once it was too late. You could stumble all the way to hell, she fretted, fall into that Sin from which you don't ever recover God's grace or care. To do it would be to set oneself on the road to perdition and no coming back. Her fear of this was a weapon in her husband George's hands. Whether in anger or boredom, my great-grandfather would sometimes make sport with Dovie's fear, telling her she'd done The Mortal Sin and thereby inspiring her to terror for her immortal soul. He'd adamantly refuse to tell the nature of the sin – he would just confidently affirm he saw her do it and feign theatrical regret that she could have acted so. Why she credited him in this, for she surely knew his character, is a story known only by her mysterious nerves. Of my great-grandmothers, Dovie is the one I wish had had a knife.

To think of Dovie inevitably leads to thoughts of George, her husband, and he works as a lesson on the way of memory. Della and Dovie stand for us as all that can be messy, all the ways the best of us may sometimes swerve a little strange. But George swerved mean, and we've paid him back by holding fast to what he would have wanted lost. He, too, is an immortal of a sort, just not the way he wished.

There's a lot to know of George, if one but wants to find it out, for he left an autobiography behind, some fifty pages he called "A Preface to My History of Life." I suppose the title indicates that there was someday more to come, but someday never came for him, so all we have is preface. It's more than plenty and, at any rate, in the choosiness of memory, we have largely chosen to ignore it. In his telling, his life was a redemption. "In my ramblin' days I had a ruff time," he writes. "Some times in danger, some times I didn't care for no one, I was with bad company. I done many things that I now regret. There was times it seemed as if I wanted a chance to shoot and kill." That does sound feisty and the sort of thing we'd like, but it's early in the pages, and the rest is duller by degrees. By his own recounting, he soon traded pistol for a Bible and settled into something better. But for all that those around him saw, though he may have lost the coarser impulse, he but settled into more studied forms of spite. What we most remember is not what tales he told himself, but what was seen, and seen by those who knew him.

George was clever, to be sure, but clever turned to others' disadvantage. His work on Dovie's nerves was just one bit of this, but there was more. For a time, George ran a general store and chose to be a cheat. He would price beans at 10¢ a can or two for 25¢, hoping thereby to part customers with low numeracy from a little more of their money. He would run meat going off through the grinder to pink it up, the better to sell spoiled as fresh to the unwitting. Our family has other cheats, but none else that cheated poor. More generally, George reveled in petty exercises of the power one person can take over another, his pleasures greatest when tinged with dominating meanness. Family memory has not forgiven this in him. Indeed, it's most of what we kept of George. I did know George – "Papa" to me – but only in the way that children know cross and elderly relatives they fear. But as I've aged, I've found him useful in his way.

In writing out his recollections of his life, George tried to tell us what of him to keep. He told the facts of things but colored them with fiction, with a character he did not have. He wanted to do work on memory, to record what we should keep. We are no historians, with fidelity to truth in all of its completeness. But neither will we submit to the purportedly heroic, to cleaner versions of ourselves, to memory that's set aright where life went wrong. My people, in short, will not be steered. The character of memory as mine have sought to do it has about it a humility that George sought to deny us. To be sure, we have an eye for the arresting and dramatic – if you will chase someone with a knife, even just once, you may need to accept that this will stick with others. But the broader logic running through what we keep answers not to drama, but to frailty. None of us succeed in ever-stable self-control. Temper, nerves, or even bowels will sometimes defeat the best of us. Incontinence is not the steady way of things, but still it happens to us all. And there is a good in keeping this, I find.

When I turn away from family and back to my work among the Greats of philosophy, I find it reassuring that all that labor to keep alive the wise and best is not the only labor that I do. All the academic work I do will matter not to mine. They'll find and keep instead some moment I swerve out from that. I can't predict what it might be – we none of us control what lasts – but it will almost surely be some humbling oddity, some mortifying monument to weaknesses of temperament or will. This is a consolation, of course, for when incontinence may come. In doing odd, I'll but be doing as my ancestors did, and it's easier to tolerate the sacrifice of dignity where it joins one firmer to a company of one's own. So too, when I am gone, what will be kept will be the liveliest, I think. When the dead are only respectable and seemly, they truly do seem dead. Impressive immortal achievements be damned, maybe it's better that someone remembers your trots and passes the tale along, preserving you from the deadening of a dignity none of the living possess.

25

The Last Start

Among the material inheritances I have from my grandmother is a bread start. For the uninitiated, some breads begin with a fermented yeast mixture, a mixture that must be maintained over time to achieve its chemical and flavoring effect for the eventual bread. Sourdough bread is like this, the justly earned "sour" in its name derived from the fermentation of its start. My grandmother's start is for "Amish Friendship Bread," a sweet, cinnamon-sugar loaf that we all conspire to call "bread" in order to excuse eating cake for breakfast. I am doubtful that the Amish have anything to do with it and suspect the appellation of "Amish" indicates an assumption rooted in the nature of the bread: This is a bread requiring so much care that it must have originated with a people accustomed to the devotions of work.

When Grandma gave me the start, it was accompanied by a carefully written set of instructions. The goal in using a start well is to use it, but never use it up. It needs to be, as my grandmother put it, "kept going," and this entails a ten-day process that was detailed in my instructions, with each day accompanied by a command, typed emphatically in all-capital letters. Some days one needs but to STIR WITH A WOODEN SPOON. Other days, one needs to add milk and sugar to the mix. Mercifully, most days only require DO NOTHING. I did ask whether it indeed matters that the spoon used to stir it be wooden and Grandma gravely answered that she didn't know but that I best not take any chances by using stainless steel. On the tenth day, one is left with a start that has multiplied. A start for one baking has, through an alchemy of additional ingredients and fermentation time, become four. This power of multiplication is what makes the result *friendship* bread, for, as my instructions insist, once armed with four starts, I should bake one, give two to friends, and retain the last to begin the entire process anew. My grandmother's multiplication of her own start is how I got mine. And when she gave it to me, it was clear that the start was indeed like friendship usually is – a blessing, but also a heavy burden.

Grandma did not make the original start herself and did not know how it was made. It had been given to her by a friend (of course). So on giving a start to me, she impressed upon me that it was irreplaceable. If not maintained, I would not be able to recreate it, no more could she. She had tended her own for decades and could, in case of disaster, re-supply me with another. But this was not an option either of us could wish. I knew that if I failed the start, failed to keep it going, my grandmother would begrudge me such a waste. She had done so with my sister-in-law. Maribeth had dramatically failed her own start, and recounting this offense was part of Grandma's recitation of instructions for my own. It was a cautionary tale not to be ignored.

Maribeth had so enjoyed eating Amish bread that she innocently asked for the recipe. So Grandma gave Maribeth both a start and the written commands to keep it going. Some months later, as she would, Grandma inquired after it. With a horror that would abide for the rest of her days and rear up afresh any time Amish bread was mentioned in her presence, Grandma learned that Maribeth had thrown the start away. Most egregiously, she had done so because "it reeked." Maribeth was right of course – start does smell foul. So, too, it looks foul, a muddy sludge that, over the ten-day cycle, achieves a variety of appearances, each a bit worse than the previous. Fermentation is just like that, but Maribeth did not know and thus had tossed it out, assuming something in the mixture had gone wrongly, badly off. Grandma never quite forgave her this. For Maribeth had, in professing her disgust, inadvertently trod on one of my grandmother's most stubborn and formidable qualities: her pride.

My grandmother's pride was general – her esteem for herself and all that was hers rooted in the usual sorts of things, such as being a good and decent person, behaving respectably and well. But the vulnerabilities of her pride were not general. They instead lodged intractably in having been poor and in being "farm" rather than "town," or, more accurately, in how being "farm" could be taken by others as being rough, uncivilized, and unrefined, and, above all, as dirty.

Before I was born, a cousin who lived a city life paid a visit to my grandparents on the farm. During a supper Grandma had prepared with her customary meticulous care, this cousin remarked with revolted amazement the abundance of flies on the farm. As her own dignity required, Grandma politely soldiered on through the remainder of the visit, but this cousin was henceforth rendered into outraged legend. For the worst insult anyone could deal Grandma was to suggest that she or her home were dirty, that anything about her person, her place, or anything belonging to her was a source of disgust or revulsion owing to any uncleanness. She was not just clean, she was defiantly so. She naturally understood that flies are dirty and unpleasant – this explained her utterly inhuman skill with a flyswatter – but to see and announce out loud the trouble of flies was to insult her lifetime of effort to keep a pristine house on a dairy farm, to be as good as "town" in country. It was not an affront she could forgive, especially as it was delivered over her very own table.

In remarking her disgust at the start, then, Maribeth had implicated Grandma in preparing food that contained material so foul it could be taken as spoiled. So, too, I expect Maribeth inadvertently struck the rawest of all of Grandma's nerves, the sore spot where her dislike of being thought dirty joined up with the thrift instilled in her by poverty. She was not dirty, but neither did she waste, a conjunction of habits hard to maintain. She never discarded milk that was blinky, that souring state just tipping into spoilt, and was expert at cutting away any offending bits on an ear of corn in order to save the worthy rest. To have her start cast off as rotten, then, summoned up the full magnitude of her pride when injured. Maribeth had discarded something she would happily have used herself, and not only was it rejected, her happiness in using it was made suspect, as if she could not recognize as others would what is too foul to cook. I bore all of this in mind in the years that followed, as I managed my own foul and unlovely start.

Since receiving my start, I have baked countless loaves of Amish Friendship Bread, though I have never yet passed on a start to any friend. I don't trust myself to be myself if I give away a start. I might succumb to echoing my grandmother, to give as I was given. I would enjoin – how could I not? – to take care against stainless steel spoons. And I might ask after the start when time had passed, wondering how it's getting along, as if it is a puppy I have entrusted to another's care. More basically, there are none among my friends I can imagine would want one or who, at any rate, would want to caretake a fermented mixture that, if done right, will endure for decades.

Part of what has sustained my own efforts is that start can be frozen. I have mercifully not needed to calendar the intervening years in blocks of ten-day fermentation cycles but have instead frozen my start so that I can initiate the process when I will and when my life permits. This lightens, but does not relieve, the burden of my start.

After Grandma died, I cleaned out her deep freeze. By then, her days of cooking had already been consumed by the frailty and illness that preceded her end. So although her freezer did contain several starts, these too had died. Start cannot survive a freezer indefinitely – whatever mysteries of chemistry attach, it will lose its motive power if kept too long without refreshing. I did not then rue the loss of Grandma's starts for I had my own and assumed there must be others in the family, other kin who also had their starts. But I was wrong about this. Whether there were once more starts in the family, there are no longer; there are no more of Grandma's starts than mine.

It is dreadful to possess the last of the starts. A few years ago when a power outage ruined the contents of my freezer, I took care to initiate the ten-day cycle precisely to keep the start alive and intact. I was once alarmed to discover that I let too much time pass between cycles and so my bread lacked the lift it ought properly to have. I then commenced a series of experiments with yeast additions. These did the trick and restored the start to its proper state. But each brush with the mortality of starts leaves me newly burdened. If I fail now, it will all be over and there will not be any more.

Food is a transitory pleasure; what delights it may offer are kinetic and passing. This is just the way of this species of pleasure. Indeed, part of the value of especially good food is just its fragile, fleeting nature – one delights in a fine meal not least because it is not a commonplace endlessly and prosaically repeated. But there is something altogether different in losing the power to generate such transitory delight. To finish a loaf one has made is just the way of bread and one that cannot be regretted – the last of a loaf is rarely the best and one is usually ready to be done with eating it for a time. But only for a time. To be done with all the loaves forever is an ending of a different order, the transient made melancholy and given finality. Even so, I sometimes want to wail: Must I make this bread forever?

I may yet fail the start, I know, and while this would offer a relief of sorts, it is not an ending I can like. I place no store in the dead surviving and abiding to witness the doings of the living who outlast them, but neither am I easy with my own imagination, of what I know my grandmother's disappointment would be. Part of her pride, as well as her injury in being thought dirty, derived from her own radical competence. She was a woman who managed much, terribly much and all at once. So to fail the start, to find it dead through mere neglect, would be, through some alchemical process of transferred meaning, to fail her in some basic way. To be sure, I lack her formidable competence, but this is all the more reason to *keep it going* in this one small way. Surely I can do this at least and not let just any start, but all starts hence, be wasted from neglect.

A better end, I sometimes think, would be to kill the start, to have done with it deliberately. In my fanciful imaginings, I conceive a funerary feast for the bread itself, the last bite of the last loaf remarked with ceremony and a formal leave-taking. Indeed, as a bit of mourning, this would well answer some of my sorrows, a way to make symbolic potency from a failure purposive and deliberate. For I have now outlived not just Grandma but also Maribeth. So maybe I can reimagine the burden of this bread. It can be noble to bear burdens, but maybe it takes real guts to lay them down. Maribeth was good at this. However abiding my grandmother's dismay at her waste of start, Maribeth stood upright where she had shuffled off: *You know,* she would explain with unflinching, wry resolve, *it really did reek.* To kill the start could be my lonely sisterly salute, a message from living to dead that says: I just won't do it either – however fine the bread, I will not keep this foul and unlovely mixture going for the rest of my mortal life.

Some day, I think, I really will do it. I will slay the start. I simply have to sort and order what exactly I want it most to mean when I resolve that this bread ends with me and I decree that there shall be no more. Till then I keep it going, this friendless "friendship" bread, and as the years go by, it becomes like carrying loneliness itself.

26

Once the Roof Goes

One of the cardinal rules of writing is that you should seek to show, not to tell. It's better for your writing and, especially, for any reader, if you don't club them with exposition that plainly articulates just what they need to understand. Instead, you should seek atmospheric description that allows a process of discovery and revelation, interpretation that allows a kind of feeling-along-with what transpires on the page. While this rule is avidly observed in the best of literature, philosophers are schooled against it.

In philosophy writing, you want to lead right away with the thesis or (in a word I have come to despise) the *point.* A philosopher once explained our writing ethos by saying that if a philosopher was writing a murder mystery, the first page would say something along the lines of "in this book, I will show that the butler did it." I have used that quip so often in teaching philosophy writing that I despair of myself for it. The students need to know the form, but I confess that I miss the chaotic style of work I sometimes got before I learned better how to instruct their writing, those essays that veered and careered all over the place only to end up somewhere unpredictable and weird. Perhaps because I now struggle so much to write at all, I am all sympathy with the fevered confusions of my early students, their tendency to start work with no real idea of where it is going and the ways their work would just collapse into *something* at the end. The essays weren't so much finished as ended – with a "conclusion" because one was needed, but not necessarily with a conclusion that had a lot to do with what came before. Sometimes, you just have to stop wherever you've landed and tack on whatever you can, so that's what they did.

I want here to write something about the crumbling one-room schoolhouse that sits atop a fine hill near my farm. That school *matters* to me, both as a physical structure and as a symbolic totem, though of what I struggle to say. I wish to write of it because it matters to me, but I struggle to write of it, also because it matters to me. I would like not to foul it up or get it wrong. I worry that my powers of show are unequal to it, and I worry that my philosopher's training to tell will spoil it, reduce it to some altogether tedious *point*. Better, then, I think, just to say something of it in the style of my early students. Write what you will and end up where you do.

The Fruitville School – for this is its name – is the last and increasingly shabby remainder of a quixotic scheme devised by one Jay L. Torrey. Born in 1852, Colonel Torrey, as he is called around here, was a lot of things in his life: a soldier, a lawyer, a cattleman. He led Torrey's Rough Riders during the Spanish-American War and was once considered a possible candidate for vice president, though Teddy Roosevelt beat him out for that. He was originally from Wyoming, but he ended up in our area, founding Fruitville Farms in 1906. During that period, the area was having a bit of a boom, lively with agricultural commerce and trains coming through to carry away our fruit to buyers elsewhere. The small towns nearest us, all with populations below two hundred now, were going concerns, filled with fruit pickers and packers. Perhaps because things were bustling or just because the area is indeed quite fine,

Colonel Torrey decided he wanted not only to found a town but to persuade the state legislature to relocate the state capital to his new town. Since my writing can only manage so much suspense, I will here dispel some: The state capital remains where it has always been, in Jefferson City. And the "town" itself never got much past the imagined stage. Even so, the school was built and functioned as a school for some years. My grandmother taught there.

The Fruitville School stands atop a hill from which the smaller hills and valleys all round are visible and where it must have caught every cold wind in winter. The foundation is native stone mortared in the puzzle-piece configuration common to stone buildings in the area. The school's single door faces west and its sides feature tall and closely spaced windows, presumably the better to catch all the light needed to read those ABCs in a time when electricity had not yet reached as far as us. The rear wall is solid but for an enclosed chimney, and one can still see that it must once have been painted for a chalkboard, with a rail running the length of the wall to hold chalk pieces. Until about fifteen years ago, one of the interior window facings still held an ornate small metal stand designed to hold a flag. I took what was left of that flag stand and have it in a box along with other odd bits I've picked up round the farm and surrounds. I don't know what once grew around the school, but it is shaded now by a grand old oak that, late in the day, lays its silhouette in perfect shadow against the planking walls. These, then, are its physical features, at least those that have abided through time. What else I know of it I only learned from talking to my grandmother.

When Ruby taught at Fruitville School, she was obliged to find room and board with a nearby family. In order to teach, she had to be unmarried, but being unmarried meant she also had to find a family with whom to live, for a woman living on her own, alone, was just not done. Her housing at Fruitville was far afield, and she recalled the long trek on foot, through whatever weather the world saw fit to offer, and up that tall hill to reach her school. Once there, she would need to stoke the stove with wood to warm the space and, in addition to instruction, her day would include preparing food for her pupils to eat. The region was poor but, through New Deal arrangements, the school was supplied with canned foodstuffs. This was how she and her students first came to taste pineapple, though by her later telling most of the children were unimpressed. More commonly, she just cooked beans. She said little of the teaching itself, but I can well imagine how it went, for my grandmother was always committed to the idea that poor does not mean ignorant. She would have taught those children to be well spoken and to write a good hand, for she begrudged the world its readiness to assume the worst of those who have little and thought one needed to be well armed against just this. She never told me anything she knew of particular children she taught or what later became of them, though I did once see one of her students.

When Ruby was living in a nursing home during one of her illnesses, I sat one day in the dining room with her. Ruby never cared at all for the periodic nursing home stays she suffered. She often balked at eating, so I was there to cajole and encourage, not least because the pathway back home to the farm would have to run right through her taking some steady meals, however unappetizing she found them. In the midst of my nagging, she asked me if I saw "that girl over there, the girl in the red dress." The dining room was just then heavily populated, full of wizened and wrinkled residents, but I saw no girl – indeed, already in my late thirties, I was by far the youngest person present. Frustrated with me for not seeing the girl, she finally pointed to indicate a fellow resident. The "girl" herself was now a stooped little creature with a disordered cap of uncombed, fluffy white hair, too old to be counted a "girl" to any except my grandmother, her the "girl's" teacher almost seventy years now past. I've thought of that elderly schoolgirl as I have aged toward the stretched perspective Ruby had then, the power conferred by long time to perceive people not just as they are but also as was and when youth was still upon them. I can sometimes see my daughter as the infant she once was, but it is with the old that I would really like the gift. I'd like to take in a perspective never mine in experience, to see that vast expanse of long life backwards beyond my own beginning, wed the aged present to the youthful past.

Some fifteen years ago when the schoolhouse was not yet so decayed as to pose a hazard to any within it, I stood inside for a time. I had gone there to take pictures but found the place defiant of my lens – sometimes the fragments a camera can get just register as falsehood and you're better off using your eyes and hoping memory can stick inside what a camera will miss. The light was just then at its best, the sun descended to cast long shadows through the empty doorframe. The school was gold with late daylight. So it seemed then almost possible to imagine my grandmother there in youth, done for the day with children, and at rest after her labor. The school itself would then have still kept glass in its window frames, what dust the place played host to would have come from chalk rather than the dirt road, the trusses would be concealed by ceiling and would not be refuge to the mourning doves I saw sheltering up there. Ruby would be just a teacher in her school and not yet settled into the life that she would have, the hills and valleys all stretched out to her view. The school would have been intact and whole, but all the rest, the weighty rest, was just open and undetermined, for her and for the children too. She'd not yet have conceived a world where she would share dining space in a nursing home with "that girl" come there to learn. The later world was still many, could still spin out in any of several directions.

To be clear, I did not that day in the school romanticize my grandmother, did not conceive her as a mere "young woman," blessed then with a world of possibilities awaiting her choices.

Among her many gifts was a resistance to being romanticized. She'd have been neither sentimental, nor charmed by children as such. Teaching would have been work – useful work, to be sure, but work by which to live and earn her bread, not a vocation that had her going dewy-eyed over the promises of youth and the futures she might there nourish in them. Her teaching wasn't, even then, the start of work for her. By the time she stood before her pupils, she would have labored much, despite her youth.

My grandmother was born to a family poor, their shared survival a common effort and one that even the youngest joined. By the time she was teaching, Ruby would have been an old hand at farmwork and at shopwork – her parents had by then tried both. She'd even worked as a berry picker, though at that she had already failed. As in later life, in paid employ she was too choosy with what berries she conceived as good and fit, too selective to work as fast or as badly as the job required. So when I stood in the schoolhouse imagining Ruby at rest at long day's end, that Ruby was hazy but not rosy in her youth. I could imagine her with so much before her but couldn't shake all that was already just behind her, a sense that she herself would have weighed her future with a measure that I – with my more modern sense of "youth" and more blessed sense of "possibility" – could not hope, then or really ever, to assay. If I could have spoken with her as was and before what else she came to be, I like to think I would have recognized her. She might say of her work and youth and possibilities the same she sometimes said of food that wasn't quite so good as it could be: *It's better than a dirty snowball.* This was her wry encomium for what was merely tolerable. She had in hunger eaten dirty snow, so food that is recognizable as such must be counted better than that and, moreover, announcing the tolerable as such can perform a consolation if we need one.

When you live as I do, inhabiting the place where generations past lived out their days, you're always in the traces. Wherever you stand, some one of yours also stood. They, too, paused at the window just so, seeing something like you see, turned the stubborn knob of that door, trod the path from house to barn. Ancestors aren't residents of any vague or unknown past, but people whose lives and work are embedded in all the stuffs of experience now your own. This can sometimes be a comfort, I notice. I think it so most often in our graveyard, where I tend graves just as they would also have tended graves, our sorrows not the same but, all the same, in common shared. But it has more modest manifestations too, motivating me to work when I stand in sight of the heaps of rock piled here and there across the farm. My ancestors moved all that rock to clear pasture, so I can surely muster up the will to cut brush or mow, my labor another installment in an effort stretching long before me. But the schoolhouse doesn't sit on land we own. That hill belongs to one of the big-time ranchers round here, a man with big machinery and hired hands to run it. Maybe this, too, explains why the schoolhouse is a trace I cannot seem to fully fathom. It is a place I watch, not one I walk.

In recent years, as the cares of life have mounted up, I have taken to going to the schoolhouse just to sit. I drive to the top of that high hill, there to stare across the taut barbed-wire fencing at the place my grandmother worked. I visit it at any hour that the summons comes upon me. I know its appearance at both dawn and dusk, at midnight and at noon. So, too, I have seen its aspect in a diversity of moods, my compulsion to go there answerable to no narrow need but, it seems, any of the needs – for succor or for celebration, for calm or for agitation. In this, it might just be my church.

The schoolhouse is no longer a place of youth or possibility but now an empty shell. I could climb through the wire and approach it closer, but I don't. The externality tells me all I need to know. The rancher who owns the pasture in which the school sits has no use for it, but his cattle do. In hottest summer, they mill about it, congregating in the shade it casts.

Its four corners they find a treat in any season, using the sharp angles as a place to scratch the itches they can't reach. They, or perhaps the elements, have near collapsed the wall that faces north. It bows inward like a crescent, the wall beneath one window busted in. Since the caved flooring of the place would be a hazard to a cow, the wall is mended with a stretch of goat fencing to stop them going in. Because the prospect of the land all round is from the schoolhouse fine, wakes of vultures reliably perch upon the trusses. I watch them there and have started something of a study of them. They do not perch there high just to scan for carrion they might like, but also sleep and stretch for readiness. Even when they seem to want no action then to take, they like to cast their wings broad outward, expanding their chests wide, their wingtips at their farthest reach, presumably just for the satisfaction that this brings.

There is a saying in the Ozarks, elliptical but true: *Once the roof goes . . .* No one ever finishes the thought with more than just a sigh because the rest is taken as obvious. Endings do not come at steady pace. Barns, sheds, and houses can stand for years, enduring damage to walls, windows, and even foundation. But once the roof goes, the rest of the structure will soon, and far more quickly, follow. Buildings need both cover from the elements and the restraint a roof affords – a roof does not just cover walls but holds them in their steady shape. Once the roof goes, endings find first a fast acceleration and then finality. *Once the roof goes* remarks the point from which one can't turn back. The schoolhouse roof is almost gone. I bear witness and await the day the school lays down in tumbled heaps of oak hand sawn and nailed in place by hopeful men long dead.

There is a metaphor here, if I could only find it. Or if I could pin it down. If metaphor it be, it surely references too much or not enough. Maybe here I have but scratched my back or extended out my wings. I cannot locate now a *point,* if indeed

I had one. I might have showed something. I might, almost but not entire, have prophesied an ending. I hope my roof for writing has not yet gone. But I do have doubts. Let me here, like my early students, just collapse with that.

27

Cain't Cry

I bought gas today at the ratty little gas station-cum-general store. It's a place where you might spend half an hour buying gas – maybe because the pump broke down after you paid and now you have to wait while it gets fixed or someone divines how to make a refund, or maybe the register won't open so no one can give change when all you have is a twenty, or maybe there's just a crowd. It was crowded today so I had a long idle while several men each took their turn at the counter, paying for their gas and picking up some fried chicken and potato wedges too. The gas station doubles as the only place in many miles to eat or buy food. While I was in line, I just listened to the men. Since it's June, the conversation had to be, as most are, about hay.

"You making hay?"

"Yeah, long day."

"No other kind of days but long ones making hay."

"Last year, I got a crick in my neck running the mower in June what lasted all the way through August."

"I know that crick. I done had that crick every year for the last dozen."

"Yeah, that's the one."

I started rolling my neck around, the way one does to loosen up. I had never met that crick myself, but it seemed a contagious sort of thing so best be prudent.

"You doing OK otherwise?"

"Cain't cry. Well, I can. But ain't nobody gonna wanna listen. So I figger I may as well not."

Conversations such as these did once console me. Labor that is hard is better managed with others who will share it and know what it exacts, who can commiserate and even echo your complaints. There is, in particular, something especially reassuring about deciding not to cry when one otherwise might or could, about withholding sorrows others will not heed. I'm not sure how that man might have meant it, but I took him to be remarking a kind of defiantly cheerful fatalism and the dry-eyed solidarity that might come with that when it is shared with others. His words would work a conversion on the world, making solidarity out of tears we will not shed because they will not be attended. People will not want to listen to one's weeping because they will have woes their own, not because they do not care. And, after all, my crying might well summon yours along and soon we'd all be drowned. Best to keep your finger in the dike lest we flood the world entire in our tears. Or, as that old Roman Stoic Seneca put it: "Why weep over parts of life when all of it calls for tears?"

Seneca's letters are full of bold and brave men. He speaks of warriors and philosophers who not only decline to cry but who will take the sorry stuff that fate will hand them and resolutely give a little sniff in great contempt. They are unbowed by travails that would fell others, standing erect before the onslaught of what poor fortune meanly will provide. There seems to be an Ozark version of this caught in conversations like I heard today. It's less that one will stand erect, though, than that one can laugh a bit when hard days leave you bowed. The cricks will come and some will really last, but maybe succor can be found in shrugging, wry resignation for the fact. To make light of what will weigh you down might make the weight a little less, for light and laughter are a sort of power, especially when shared. Laughter can belittle that which bows us and thereby make it shrink a bit. Seneca also said that there are some problems it is better to scorn than to solve, and perhaps there are problems better still to mock than mull.

Thoughts like these explain why I used to find consolation in the Ozark Stoics, the men who accumulate in this style of talk in gas station lines, parts counters, and the feedstore loading bay. The way they would complain just in order to make sport of all complaints was a tonic against finding any of my troubles that little bit too much, a remedy against tears it's better not to shed. That was how I heard such things before the billboards started to appear.

Out on several of the highways there are billboards now that feature an image of a farmer, his back turned to the camera, his eyes presumably directed outward toward the fields that sit in softer focus in the distance. Or maybe he is glassy-eyed and staring vacantly at the horizon, his gaze in fact turned inward on his woes while his eyes are but set in simulacrum of sight turned to the world. We cannot tell where he is really looking when all we see is his broad back. But this should be our worry. What we can't see could be a peril, and that is just the billboard's point. The signs prominently post a phone number one should promptly call "if you think he's thinking about suicide," if you think your own "he" may not last. The billboards are a gesture at what statistics about rural men lately show: they have started killing themselves in ever escalating numbers. So increased are these kinds of deaths that they have been given a name, "deaths of despair," a category intended to include not just the quick, decisive finality of suicide but the slower, grinding deaths of addiction where opioids to still the pain can all too easily still it once and for all in inadvertent overdose. Seen from the back, it's hard to tell what afflictions might sit heavy on that man in the billboard.

But then, I start to wonder, aren't all the men round here seen mostly from the back?

I am here making fast and loose with the timing of my thoughts. Before the billboards started to appear, my mind had already made this turn. There's a thing I do not wish to write, about an uncle found outside our graveyard's gates, his gun beside him and him dead. My cousin found my uncle's body on his own way to his morning chores. Then he stood by to wait the help he summoned in from town, joined there by my father and my other uncle, all three like sentries at a gate already breached. They do not speak of the time they passed there waiting. I do not know if they then cried.

Garret and I once dug a grave of sorts in our cemetery, the one that would hold my sister-in-law's ashes when my brother and his daughters brought her home to rest from where she died. Ashes do not need a big hole, but all holes are hard to dig upon that hill. My brother would himself perform the proper burial, with his small daughters, when they could do it out of sight of others. But I wanted in my grief to make the spot a ready place, to make sure, before my brother and those tiny girls laid a shovel to the land, that the place that she would rest was empty. Our graveyard is old and there are unmarked graves inside it. My grandfather used to recall digging a grave there in his younger years, saying of the digging that "we hit coffin and had to move over." I did not want my brother hitting coffin. The work was hard and miserable – the spot was empty of any dead but was all over stone and rock. I cried throughout, and I remember thinking then that here is the worst and saddest thing that I have ever done or will do. But I have since learned that one cannot really count on such conclusions.

There is a necessary self-sufficiency demanded of people who live a distance from help or town. Things that people nearer help might be able to avoid are unavoidable. Things that people nearer help might not have to do themselves, we do ourselves. So you end up doing things you wouldn't think you would have in you. For me, this has included letting go of any sense that I have yet done the worst that I will do.

Garret and I were not at the farm when my uncle died, but we made haste to get there just as soon as we learned of it. After passing what words could pass between us and the rest, we went up to the graveyard. The spot where my uncle died looked little changed, the gate itself the simple sort it long has been. Someone, likely my cousin, had cleared the space, though this, too, is something never spoken of. At a look, you could now think it a place where nothing more than the usual griefs of graveyards had transpired. But Garret and I stood and stared, and stared long enough to see it wasn't so. Small blood still marked the silver of the fence and larger in a pool gathered in a low spot facing east.

It's hard to know what to do with a pool of blood spilled far from water, not even with a tool on hand. It needs sacralizing, sanctifying. But it also needs to be hid and quick – we would not be the only ones to stand there in our sorrow, and the ground needed making *right*, like ground that one could walk on, like ground solid beneath feet and not a low spot ready to gape open and drown us all in sorrow. So Garret and I buried that blood with our bare hands, just piled up earth to first absorb and then conceal it. Not a hole to dig as worst, but worse than digging a hole had been. My memory of my uncle's blood has stuck around, but little of the rest that passed that day has done. I do not remember if we cried.

The summer after this, I encountered a truck wrecked on the highway near our farm. Right before you reach our road, there is a wicked turn and alongside it a steep decline. The truck had missed the curve and careered downhill to crash at speed against a fencepost. I arrived just as another driver ran down the hill to try to offer aid. The man in the truck was both alone and elderly, blood spilling from his head and yet still conscious with it. We made haste to call for help, but it would take almost three-quarters of an hour before the help would come. With another call, made to my mother, we began to try to track down his kin. We learned then that he was from nearby and himself fresh with grief, a widower of just two days old. These efforts soon gave way to others, as the injured man tried to leave his truck, his body unable but his mind confused enough to try. Because his eyes were beclouded by the blood then spilling from his head, I took off my shirt and used it as a compress, an effort feeble for this purpose but one that helped all the same to hold him in his place. Time passed. Help was long enough in coming that my shirt was soon defeated and the overcoming blood just gathered into pools inside my hands. Time passed. When my hands were overcome, it just ran down my arms and dripped from my elbows onto his blue jeans. Time passed. Then we heard the ambulance and at last surrendered the old man to better sorts than we ourselves could be. I learned that evening that the old man died and that his wife's funeral would now be joined with his. Throughout it all, I did not cry.

I have started to go dry-eyed, though not yet a person seen only from the back.

28

Signs and Portents

A few nights back, Garret found Jason, the rancher who leases pasture from us, in a mood most foul. A newborn calf had gone missing. It was coming on to dark and Jason had been out searching, fruitlessly.

Calves do not stray far all on their own. Find where the mother lurks and lows, and the calf will be nearby, slipped through a gap of fence, most likely. But the mother was with the herd, silent and complacent as the rest. Nor were there signs or marks of some worse fate, no blood or remains to tell on a coyote, no vultures hovering near to finish what another creature started. The calf was simply gone, as if it had never even existed, the only trace of it a heifer who but yesterday was sore pregnant, now empty and all done with that. No one can enjoy a mystery such as this. Newborn calves are vulnerable to all manner of ills and troubles, but they do not simply disappear.

Underneath all my philosophical training, my ostensible commitment to a life of reasoning and argumentation, a tendency to wary superstition still has lurked. Time on my farm has only strengthened this. Who, after all, can pass by a hawk killed upon his collision with a run of barbed-wire fencing, his wings extended for flight but now snagged in chilling crucifixion, and not experience a tremor of disquiet? Such things fairly demand to be seen as omens, or at least as visitations of the humility that should be the proper human lot. I would take it as a loss were I never more arrested into raw, brute feeling at the appearance of some natural marvel, if I could not be abducted into wonder or foreboding. Whether the world, itself and in fact, delivers signs and portents, I cannot say. I only know that if it does, I don't want to miss them. My family's late troubles have turned this tendency to burden.

There is no shortage of empirical facts about my father's recent decline. Indeed, I can recite them all by heart and have by now too often done so. When we visit the doctors, I am the family voice, the one to detail all that is and can be known. But my recitations are like the ones that a medieval peasant would make, a catechism offered up in Latin by one who does not know that language. I voice the words, not in understanding but rather like so many hopeful incantations that may prove belief and thus provoke, at last, some kind of answer. I make sounds that may yet, if we are lucky, summon up some meaning. Doctors mostly thrive on language I don't speak, nor do they adopt the tongue that I would have them take. What do all the myriad sad and sorry facts *add up to* for one who lives, or who will die, with them? They do not say. So I supplement my orthodox recitations with a too keen eye upon the wilder world I find in operation at the farm. I look avidly for signs.

Too many things are lately not where they belong.

Last week there was a cow slipped through taut fencing, grazing by the curving highway. She was just at that terrible corner where some years ago that old man crashed his truck and died, as if positioned there where fate could most easily have its way with yet another come too fast around the bend.

Just days ago, Garret watched the elusive fox we only rarely glimpse idling at leisure in our yard. That fox has only ever been a creature caught in glancing sight and from the corner of an eye. But he is no longer something you can only think you might have seen. He is now spectre made fully formed and even casual with it, a thing to see straight on.

Even the branches of one of our finest walnut trees have not stayed where they belong. They have begun to drop in sizes and in numbers that make the shade it casts a hazard one cannot enjoy. We have begun to warn visitors never to park beneath it and ourselves try not to stand or pass within its reach for long.

Some couple of weeks ago, when swans turned up in the lake at the back of our farm, I inwardly sighed in some considerable relief. If, for the first time in living memory, we have come to host those majestic, graceful creatures, some breath of fate may yet blow fair not foul. But those swans are gone now or, rather, all but one has gone. The one remaining is scattered in pieces upon a lovely rise of hill, the white of those vast wings stark against the green and feathers cast across long yards of distance. It must have been a terrible fight to leave them flung so.

And now this calf. When Garret tells me of it, it seems the most convincing of our recent signs, an ill omen that at once exceeds and confirms all. Things are out of order, and this the portent to show most decisively it is an out of order to favor misfortune. Unlike all the others, it is not a visitation proper. It is a visitation of an absence, a gap and emptiness where these rightly should not be. It is an empirical fact, and one I can say in language all my own, that calves do not simply disappear.

Calves do not simply disappear. And, as it happened, this one didn't. Jason later found its corpse, bloated and floating in the pond. It never lived to stand or step, for its mother birthed it there, beneath the murky waters. The mystery of the missing calf is "solved," absence resolved into a horrifying presence – a presence Jason used chains and tractor to move elsewhere and away from what the cows would drink.

Cows, I would have thought until just now, surely know what they are about when they give birth. At least, one wouldn't birth a calf in water that would drown it on the instant it emerged. But this one did. This is a fact, a truth to which we can in confidence cling. But it isn't one that any here can use. Some facts do not demystify, the explanation they provide bereft of meaning or of wanted sense. A gap in my understanding has closed; another one now opens.

29

Death Just Got Out of This Truck

Maybe we should just skip the middle step and throw it all straight in the toilet? This is what I ask my mother as we together stand and consider the overburdened farm table. We are bereaved, and so a steady stream of neighbors has come by to deliver casseroles and pies, lunch meats and cookies, chicken and potato salad. If death were an appetite, we'd have the means to satisfy and send him off by now. But he is not an appetite, nor have we any of our own.

Mine are a people of uneasy stomachs. I remember one night spent in the ER alongside some uncles and cousins, waiting to hear what the doctors would make of my grandfather's alarming stroke-like swoon. That night we shared the TUMS bottle the way others might pass a flask. Bringing food to us bereaved is like giving a dog a pencil. There's just not much that we can do with it, at least not much that anyone could count useful.

Grief is an affliction physical and material. It roils the gut and stops the sleep. It can put a tremble in the limbs, a quiver in the voice, a restless agitation run all through. It makes the knees want to let go, the body just to sink. It is tired but cannot ever really rest, a breath you cannot really catch. It can make the gaze go vacant, blank. Grief is eyes that see too much, make sense of little. How long have I now stared out the window into nothing, seeing nothing? Grief sets the body all awry. The body *wants*, but what? Something it can now no longer have, a voice in the ear gone mute, a touch tactile, now but memory. We stare at food; we do not eat it.

My book on death, the one I will not write, was originally going to have a chapter on the body. It seemed to me that one of the troubles with philosophy on grief is that it misses out on bodies. The philosopher's talk is all of what loss means, what grief can make you think. It speaks to what the mind and heart may feel, but not the stalling, empty mind or trembling heart. It speaks to one who speaks and thinks, not the instinctive, aching animal, not the raw creature all sensation without sense. This is not a novelty where philosophy is concerned – philosophers have long neglected the cruder materiality from which thought transpires. But still, I wanted some way to make philosophy answer not to thought or feeling or meaning, but to the brute stuff upon which all the rest is set. I wanted some way to make loss less like an experience of the mind and thought, to make loss on the page more like itself in life, an experience altogether *nauseating*. Before the reasoning or meaning, first the gut.

There are, I find, things I want philosophy to do that it cannot. Or that I cannot do with it. There is nothing wrong with thought, with seeking out some sense. But what can be made sense is rarely all there is; it leaves in remainder much, too much. Worse still, even good sense can be misleading. You can get your thoughts in careful order, root out all mistakes, prepare to read the vexations of experience with well-honed training pitched to make vexations yield. But all that practiced thought and careful habits of the mind can leave you unready for what comes. Don't trust them more than they can bear. The body is not a prison, but neither can thought escape its meaty and substantial bonds. I cannot make philosophy bend to this, I think, not in a way that is not all false and false confidence.

Many years ago now, when the farm was still a working dairy and the place was hectic with cows and work, my grandfather hired a milker to come in and help. The milker had a love of the drink and would sometimes cry off work for a hangover, but he was, I suppose, reliable enough that they kept him on. One day, he'd taken the farm's yellow truck into town to retrieve some feed. At a four-way stop sign, he was briefly bested by a fancy man in a fancy car, the kind of man who didn't want to wait on a beater truck that got there first and instead just blew the stop sign so he'd get ahead. The milker would have none of this, so he drove that yellow truck right up to and behind the man's bumper for blocks that soon turned into miles. Finally, the fancy man pulled over in a parking lot, the milker close behind. Both men got out of their vehicles. The fancy man planted his feet wide and bellowed out a caution meant to be severe: *I have to warn you that I just got out of karate!* The milker didn't even pause before he answered quietly, *Well, I just got out of this yellow truck.* Before aught else could happen, the milker's fist had found that fancy man and laid him flat.

Karate class is fine and so, too, is philosophy. But make no mistake, you can't really get ahead of it. Loss comes at you like a fist.

30

Decoration Day 2025

I have a corner full of false flowers I need to make tidy. They are the stuffs for my annual offerings to our dead. Monday is Decoration Day, the day that my family observed the old custom of cleaning up the graves of our dead and laying them fresh with new flowers. This year I have bought a radical excess of false flowers. They sit in tangled heaps where I left them in a corner and where they have reproached me for the last two weeks. I bought earlier this year than usual, wanting to find the best and having conceived a plan more ambitious than years prior. I won't just clean and decorate the graves we have in years most lately passed – my grandparents, my sister-in-law, and my uncle. I will reach back farther, and lay for my great-great-grandparents, my great-grandparents, and also for their lost infants. Those babies would have been my grandfather's elder siblings had they lived more than the mere days fate meanly gave them. One is laid in our family cemetery, buried there by her own parents and for years marked only by a plain rock. The other is laid in a double burial, with a distant uncle or cousin, in another small rural cemetery nearby. When families in our area could not afford a plot, they sometimes laid kin with kin, and that is how my great-grandparents buried their firstborn. I will place flowers for that infant boy and all the rest, at least this year.

My reproachful heap of false and admittedly somewhat garish flowers could be taken as testament to some old and unresolved discomfort with the facts of loss. Why, after all, resurrect for remembrance dead so long lately unremarked? Like people themselves, memory has a natural lifespan. The graves that wear flowers and tokens on Decoration Day are also the newest, their ornamentation a trace of "life" in those most lately dead. We decorate for those we can ourselves recall; the oldest parts of any cemetery are also the barest, for it is there where rest the dead who have died their second death, the end that comes when no one living knows you. In laying flowers for my distant kin, I will violate the natural order and bring back dead already gone. In my defense, I am lonely and could use the company.

For generations my family reliably observed Decoration Day the way it ought to be and always was. We did not just tidy graves but picnicked with our dead, gathered up in happy crowds around homemade food set up on clumsy tables brought to the graveyard for this purpose. But that has stopped, the tradition ended now with us.

I am in most ways a person without religion, yet I harbored a faithful commitment to Decoration Day. Some few years ago, I wrote a kind of essay in praise of it, of my family's habitual and somewhat shambolic behavioral recitation of the archaic ways. I didn't know it then, but when I wrote of it we had already celebrated our last such day in the graveyard. I have been in mourning ever since. If Decoration Day itself could have a grave, I would cut to the chase and lay all my false flowers there.

Sometimes it is just "the way of things" that things can't last. Yet I find this wholly unsatisfying as an explanation, much less succor for a loss. "The way of things," I find, is only ever cited in disappointment and sadness. At least, I can't recall ever being told "it's just the way of things" when good has been my lot. It is a phrase for consolation, not congratulation, a phrase for just those "things" we wouldn't in our agency make so. Nonetheless, some of our late failures to observe Decoration Day might just be called "the way of things." Some of the living who would otherwise walk the ancestral tracks and gather up at graves have been flung by fate away. Our neighborhood has been thinned out, the way most small farming communities have. As elders died, children sold up or had to find work elsewhere. So, too, some who might once have come have grown too aged and too frail to make their way there. These sorry facts are indeed just "the way of things," however little that may please us. But while "the way of things" could but have thinned our ranks, it is the pandemic that finished us entire.

In May of 2020, as Decoration Day approached, my branch of the family tree agreed together that we ought not gather up. My parents and an uncle were all in that benighted class of those counted specially vulnerable, so caution seemed the better course. We would stay away and told the others of our kin of this decision. I do not know if they then gathered anyway, if they held tradition fast despite its risks. I only know they disagreed and deeply so. One cousin sent my parents a letter describing the pandemic as a "righteous culling" performed by God, a test of faith my parents then were failing. And so began a breach never yet mended. During those first several months of the pandemic, my kin divided and have stayed so. To be sure, we carry on a pretense of sociability when circumstance puts us together, but our days of sharing table and of fond and cheerful intercourse have passed. I have a cousin that used reliably to stop and talk when he passed by our lane and saw us out. It is now a toss-up as to whether he will wave as he drives fast by.

When Decoration Day of 2021 arrived, my family did go up to the graveyard, laden with our picnic fare as we had done before. But none others then arrived. We carried on despite this, but the next year didn't even try. That last effort had not felt the way it should: it felt not like a picnic or a ritual, but instead like a sorry, mundane lunch we had relocated up the hill. Decoration Day had been a day for sorrows shared, for continuity collectively asserted and with a bit of cheer. *We abide*, the Day had seemed to say, but can no longer say in earnest. So it is that I have come this year to try for resurrection, not of the Day but of my distant dead. I am already disappointed with my plan.

There is a story by Henry James – "The Altar of the Dead" it's called. It's about a man named Stransom who can't let his dead lie. He begrudges living others their forgetfulness, their habit of just going on when death comes for one they love, and pities those, their dead, then left behind. Of these forgotten dead, he says, "they asked so little that they got, poor things, even less, and died again, died every day, of the hard usage of life." Stransom doesn't stop with pity but engineers a chapel all his own. He sets upon an altar there a candle for each one he knows who dies, a humble thing that grows apace as Stransom ages and more of those he's known now die. In short, he creates a religion all his own. And as such endeavors may be wont to do, it takes a turn toward odd. He begins to feel the sort of things he really never should, his accumulating dead becoming boon:

> Various persons in whom his interest had not been intense drew closer to him by entering this company . . . There were hours at which he almost caught himself wishing that certain of his friends would now die, that he might establish with them in this manner a connection more charming than, as it happened, it was possible to enjoy with them in life.

As the years of Stransom's life and his devotion pass, he is joined in his quixotic observance by another who would mourn, a woman with a loss about which he long speculates, only at belated last to learn the truth. Hers is one dead whom Stransom knew but for whom he had refused to lay a candle, a man who had wronged him and so had been excluded – Stransom with his altar now a god who levies judgment. And there the "religion" all his own must find its end, collapsed in ritual performed alongside, but never really shared, with another. There is a lesson here I'd like to heed if only I could make it out.

Stransom makes himself the keeper and the shepherd, his flock too dead then to resist. Where the living won't be herded, the dead oblige, and this just might be the problem. We can make of them what we will, and what we like. And we can make ourselves their hero, our attentions to them the fragile tether against their second and most final death. Grief can be a form of narcissism, remembrance just the same. This may be a fault made worse where dead are "known" but through stories handed down, where the dead one never knew in life itself can also never then be really missed. I can imagine with what sorrow my great-grandparents set their babies down into the earth, but neither those babes, nor the agony in which their spare days ended, are mine in more than this. I did not know them, and I did not know their parents. They aren't entirely abstractions, but they could be something like – ancestors whose land I work because they saw a babe at last survive, a baby grown to man and father, then grandfather and great-grandfather, then himself also to the grave. They are in this sense mine, but I want not to be a Stransom with it. I want not to keep them just because they're dead while those still living have come to vex me so. Nor am I easy with the "system" I somehow now have made.

In my ancestral lineage in these parts, I have a considerable company of dead, but did not think to provision all with my false flowers. I drew a line arbitrary – I will go to that lonely little cemetery where the baby boy is laid but not some longer miles north to where my earliest kin round here are laid. I likewise wasn't planning to lay anything for that great-great-uncle, the brother to whom my great-grandfather didn't speak for years. Nor have I anything for cousins – once- and twice- and thrice-removed – those cousins I could call just "Legion." One must draw a line *somewhere*, but, really, where? And why? How does one avoid becoming like a god with it? At least the line I laid unthinking is, unlike Stransom's, not a punitive gesture. But does it help that much to admit that it is budget, both of money and of spirit? Those false flowers, however garish and awful they appear, do not come cheap. As for spirit, I cannot really say why I think a budget must be kept, but so it is. One wants not to dilute one's dead by making them too many. I can with a spirit somewhat hearty commend those dead who most directly led me where I am, to this homeplace where their feet and now mine most trod. My bigger problem, and the one I cannot solve, is not a misplaced hope for memorial heroics featuring myself as savior of my dead. My problem is with ritual itself, the way that one can neither keep nor make it all oneself.

Some years ago, at my university, the president laid into a concrete walkway a large medallion with the university's seal. It was just that kind of thing that universities sometimes produce – a bit of self-exaltation and shared spirit meant to ornament a spot. But when the medallion was placed, the president announced that here was the start of a new "tradition" – no students should walk across the medallion until that day they graduate. This announcement failed utterly to do the trick intended. Undergraduates trod across that seal daily on their tired way to classes, unaware of the "tradition." I myself biked over it every chance I got, just because I rejected then, and now, "tradition" installed by abrupt fiat. Not to be daunted in their effort, the university finally had hard iron pillars and chain fencing set around the seal. They roped it off, presumably the better to dramatically unleash this, our new "tradition," on graduation day, when they would only then allow those qualified to step across and on it. As much as I disdained that effort, I have somehow stumbled into something like.

I could place my flowers now, or any day I choose. But I withhold them, leaving them in disordered piles as if they are a thing to be unleashed, as if I would thereby and only on my lonely Day reward my chosen dead, like Stransom with his candles. My false flowers await the Day because I'm trying to make some salving new tradition where the one I'd want is lost. Our old tradition once, but no longer, made a sort of sense. We abided once, but no longer. *We abide* turned into *I abide*, but how, and as exactly what?

31

Anything at All

Some few years ago now, I sold my old white truck for scrap. I had long kept the passenger floorboard stocked with jumper cables, oil, power-steering fluid, and that one wrench helpful for adjusting the loose battery connection. In this way, I had managed never to get stranded in it. But finally there came a time when what I poured in it just poured right out again, and I had to give it up and give it over. When no one in town would take it, I used the internet to find a scrap buyer. And this is how a tow-truck driver from a city some few hours away came to arrive at the farm to carry it off.

The tow-truck driver had clearly never been in a place like this. Emerging from his truck, he stood in the dirt road, then spun himself in a slow circle to take in all around. He asked if I *lived* here, in a tone akin to awe. Well, yeah, I said, gesturing to the cabin just behind me, a place clear made for living. For the rest of his short visit, as he hooked and hoisted up my broken truck, he marveled out loud about my place. About how there is no one in sight of us, no one in hearing, just no one at all nearby. *You can do anything at all out here,* he kept repeating, *anything at all! There is nothing to stop you from doing anything at all!* I don't know just what *all* that driver yearned to do, what activities his city neighborhood denied him, but what he said has stuck with me. Sometimes one does get arrested by what a stranger to one's life will make of it.

Just as there is nothing to stop me from doing anything at all, there is nothing out here to stop me from all manner of fanciful imagining. This explains how that tow-truck driver has in the intervening years transformed into a seer. Stories from times long past often tell of strangers from distant lands arriving at isolated villages unaccustomed to the outsider. The stranger will then be treated specially, sometimes slain as threat but sometimes honored as sage, as a knower of a kind that local folks have never yet encountered. I am an open-minded person, not one to kill a stranger, so I have made my tow-truck driver over into visitation, a wise stranger come to impart leal truth I ought not to forget. And as the communications of a seer are surely wont to do, his words have proved a heavy burden as I have tried to do the thing I was supposed to do, to write some book on death.

I tried at first to use the seer's words to coax along my book on death. If I really *can do anything at all out here*, then surely I can make this book, I thought. Like living in the country, writing, too, can be an unformed, solitary thing with no articulated shape until you give it one. It can be a radical open space to occupy and to define just as you wish. You can make words do whatever you would like, so surely I could bend some to my will. I needed but to feel, and deeply feel, that exalting freedom which the seer celebrated. *There is nothing to stop me from writing a book about death!*

The existentialists argued that freedom can work on us as trouble and torment– we're *condemned* to be free and all of that. I can see what they are after in saying so. Being free means needing to resolve upon a course, to make some choice among the options and thereby go this way instead of that. Decision gets more vexing still when you understand that what you choose in freedom often comes alongside some restraint. As it happens, if you will choose to be an academic, you don't just set off on it from scratch but join up with a path already marked and trod. There are norms, there are expectations, there are ways to be that you should try to mirror and to match. There are even forms a book on death should take. So much of life, and all its several choices, seem like this. The freedom one enjoys is just a choice of harness, picking out what yoke you'll wear. This explains why I have now for years been making clumsy furrows out of death, tugging on the plow I somehow picked. This is not the life the seer saw.

It was a mistake to convert the seer's words into a banality, into a bit of self-help for the writer – as if the vast *anything at all* should merely take the shape of doing exactly that thing an excess of schooling trained me up to do. Allowed the freedom of which he spoke, would the tow-truck driver spend it towing off more trucks? I would like to think not, and in the absence of another visitation, I choose to think not. Whatever the seer meant, it cannot be so instrumental and so plain. The seer's exaltation must contain some better meaning.

The *anything at all* of which the seer spoke must be freedom of another order. To be sure, a seer worth his salt would not fail to recognize the boundedness that life itself affords. It isn't strictly true that out here I can do *anything* at all. I remain inhibited by the laws of nature. I can start fires, but I cannot summon rain. Prudence has a role to play as well – best not start fires on the windy days lest you burn down more than what you mean to. But aside from all that nature and prudence stop, the rest really is rather wide open. Even what the seer said is like this – unfixed and indefinite, a little mysterious even, the way a seer's insight ought to be. The truths of seers wouldn't be worth the value we vest in them if they were easy to make out. So even as I puzzle over what it means and what might follow from it, I'm trying to be patient at it. If you will live by a truth you only dimly understand, it's best, I think, to take it day by day.

When *you can do anything at all*, you might not choose, on any given day, to lay down words on death. There are other possibilities. One thing I have lately done instead is laying up a lot of words on etiquette. I was re-reading an old Emily Post manual, its section on funeral etiquette, not because this was likely to be especially useful to my writing but because sometimes you find a way to shirk that is close enough to what you ought to be doing that you can pretend you are not shirking. But as I was re-reading, I decisively concluded that I didn't really need or want this book anymore. This crisp revelation generated another: I would like this book better if its pages were glued to the ceiling of my barn workshop. So that is what I have been doing. It began – as naturally it would – with just the section on funerals. But though my barn workshop is small, pages are smaller still, and so I have needed all of the etiquette – the weddings, the christenings, the dinner parties, the guidelines for addressing dignitaries and for gift occasions. I haven't yet used the special insert that proclaims that *children are people too!* but I'm sure I'll get there soon. I hope to have the work complete before I need to resort to the index though. I *can do anything at all out here*, so this is what I'm doing now.

32

The Chance of It

In one of the last years of her life, my grandmother idled away a summer afternoon with me and somehow our talk turned to childhood, and to toys. She hadn't had many as a child, she noted, but she and her siblings nevertheless found much to do. "Like what?" I asked. She offered as example that she would sometimes capture June bugs, tie a thread to a leg, and then let them fly while tethered and held fast in her hand.

Once told, this fact about my grandmother fundamentally rearranged my understanding of her or, more precisely, dislodged any assurance I once held that I already understood her. There are many things I could have imagined my grandmother doing over the course of her long life, from heroic self-sacrifice to vengeful violence – Ruby possessed an intricate character that defied easy summary – but flying bugs like tiny kites seemed altogether too quixotic and even just a bit bizarre. It is a form of play at once tinged with cruelty, given how little a June bug could enjoy it, and ornately farcical. The effort, patience, and dedication to the art that it must take are alone a reason not to bother trying. After all, one would need a fine hand with thread to pull it off without pulling off the beetle's leg entire. On hearing of it, I could only stutter out the stupidest of my thoughts and said that it sounded hard to do. She sighed and simply replied, "Well, it didn't seem so then."

When I have tried to lay to paper just what it is about bereavement that most vexes me and wrecks my peace, I have never found expressions that might suit. The ennobled language of philosophy deserts me, and I want to talk elliptically, mysteriously even. "You see," I'd write, "it's all about the June bugs my grandmother tied to strings and flew like kites." It's about the fact that she had to live long enough and talk long enough for this crucial, confounding fact to emerge. But then she could not – no one could – live long enough for all such facts to find exposure. I did not really know her. We none of us can really know another. Life is never long enough for that, for all those tethered June bugs to make their clumsy flight into our conversation and, then, into our knowing. Yet still one wants the *chance of it*. This is all we get – the chance – but it is the chance that really matters.

Acknowledgments

An earlier version of "Kill All the Chickens" appeared in *Aeon*, published under the title "The Outsider" (March 6, 2018). "The Invention of Death" appeared in *Book XI*, Issue 4. Scraps and pieces of various ideas running through the book appeared in other guises in some of the formal academic work I have done.

I've had a long career in philosophy and so have had much support from various colleagues throughout. One of the earliest was a professor in my graduate program, Ron Bontekoe, whose close eye on the quality of prose instilled in me good writing habits that have stuck. Where I have mixed metaphors, they will not have been Ron's fault. More recently, Justin Weinberg has been especially helpful in hosting or flagging my work on his widely read blog for the profession. I am, above all, indebted to Eric Schliesser. Our areas of philosophy have little overlap, but he has over the years been kindly supportive. He has also given me more critical comments, pointing out when I have overwritten something or told when I should have showed. But primarily he has abided as someone who I felt could see my alienation from the work but encourage me to make something better or more imaginative of it.

This book is only a *book* because of my editor, Ian Malcolm. In writing the pieces contained here, I had given up all thought of publishing them in any of the standard ways and had posted a few on Substack. Ian saw them there and contacted me about a book. Ian was uncommonly willing to entertain writing that was hard to characterize into a tidy genre or form, and he saw the several pieces as a single work before I did. He also had a gift for describing how the work *worked* far better than my own. His persistence is why the book now exists between covers.

I am of course greatly indebted to my family for the support they have shown me throughout my career, first as a philosopher and then later as the keeper of the farm. My mother has always been the family's historian, and I owe much of what I know of us from her, though any mistakes I will have made here are mine. My father was instrumental in a thousand different ways in our being able to keep the farm and, while he was never himself inclined to farming, he gamely enjoyed what we've gotten up to. My brother read several of the pieces in draft and can cut trees like a cartoon Tasmanian devil. And it was my daughter, with her tender heart for any stray, who first lured Dog down to our place and thus introduced me to my familiar.

Above all, I am grateful to my husband, to whom this book is dedicated, but about whom I struggle to say much. Garret features some in this book, but I write of him rarely, for he contains multitudes my words can't catch. Although he doesn't appear frequently in these pages, he is, in some more fundamental sense, on every page. While I was writing most of these pieces, he was the only reader I expected and, in this quite literal sense, the book is his.